Japanese Taupe Quilt Blocks

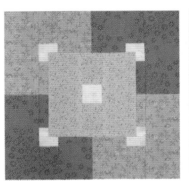  

Japanese Taupe Quilt Blocks

Calm, neutral collection

Susan Briscoe

HERBERT PRESS
LONDON · OXFORD · NEW YORK · NEW DELHI · SYDNEY

HERBERT PRESS
Bloomsbury Publishing Plc
50 Bedford Square, London, WC1B 3DP, UK

BLOOMSBURY, HERBERT PRESS and the
Herbert Press logo are trademarks of
Bloomsbury Publishing Plc

First published in Great Britain 2010
Copyright © Quarto Publishing plc, 2019

Bloomsbury Publishing Plc does not have any control
over, or responsibility for, any third-party websites
referred to or in this book. All internet addresses given in
this book were correct at the time of going to press. The
author and publisher regret any inconvenience caused if
addresses have changed or sites have ceased to exist, but
can accept no responsibility for any such changes.

A catalogue record for this book is available from the
British Library.

ISBN: PB: 978-1-78994-013-8

2 4 6 8 10 9 7 5 3 1

Conceived, edited and designed by
Quarto Publishing plc
The Old Brewery
6 Blundell Street
London N7 9BH

QUA: NQB

Editor & designer: Michelle Pickering
Art director: Caroline Guest
Illustrator: Kuo Kang Chen
Photographers: Simon Pask, Phil Wilkins
Creative director: Moira Clinch
Publisher: Paul Carslake

Printed and bound in China

To find out more about our authors and books visit
www.bloomsbury.com and sign up for our newsletters.

Contents

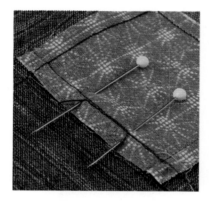

Projects

The block directory includes instructions for making six small projects.

◄ Project 2
Lap quilt, page 61

◄ Project 1
Cushion,
page 47

◄ Project 4
Table runner,
page 79

► Project 5
Wallhanging,
page 93

▼ Project 3
Tote bag, page 73

◄ Project 6
Satchel bag, page 101

Mix-and-match quilt designs

Suggestions for mixing and matching blocks are provided in the block directory on pages 39, 53, 67, 83, 89, 97 and 107.

Introduction

Many Japanese quilts are readily identifiable by their sophisticated colour schemes, beautifully patterned prints and tactile woven cottons, all in restful tones. This style has become known as Japanese taupe. This book brings together these gorgeously subtle materials with a new selection of fascinating block patterns drawn from traditional Japanese designs – all you need to create your own Japanese quilt.

TAUPE FABRICS

▼ **Grandmother's haori (kimono jacket)**
This contemporary jacket shows the sophisticated neutral colours considered appropriate for older women. The easy-care polyester fabric imitates traditional silk. Taupe fabrics include similar designs and colour schemes, which nostalgically remind many older Japanese people of their mother's and grandmother's kimono. Block 30 combines similar shades.

Japanese taupe spirit

The peaceful colours of taupe fabrics are seen everywhere in Japan, from the greyed shades considered appropriate for a grandmother's kimono to the natural colours of traditional interiors; from the glazes used for handmade ceramics to the tranquil earthy tones of the countryside in early winter. Edo-era sumptuary laws that prohibited commoners from wearing brightly coloured clothing encouraged a kind of chic understatement in colour, pattern and texture known as *iki*, and this more subdued style is regarded as a sign of good taste even today. Japanese aesthetic values – such as *kanjaku* or tranquillity, shown in fabrics as a sense of restfulness with cool, dark tones; or *shiori*, an affection for nature that may

BLOCK 30

be expressed in warmer sepia tones with a hint of luminosity—are reflected in the taupe fabric palette. The many grey colours among taupe echo dry rock gardens. *Wabi*, the understated elegance of rustic simplicity embodied in the tea ceremony, may also be experienced through taupe materials. Taupe fabrics express something of the inner feelings of Japan.

Japanese taupe characteristics

- Subtle use of colours and patterns.
- Mixing and matching blocks.
- Using assorted fabrics for a 'scrap quilt' look.
- Mixing plaids and stripes with prints.
- Avoiding plain fabrics.
- Adding embroidery and embellishments.
- Combining appliqué with patchwork.

Traditional Japanese patterns

The taupe patchwork fabrics originally created in Japan and now seen worldwide are used in many ways by Japanese quilters, often in traditional American patchwork or appliqué blocks. Popular blocks echo many traditional Japanese designs, and the blocks in this book are sourced from these Japanese originals, including kamon (family crests), kasuri (ikat) woven fabrics, Japanese architectural motifs, classical patterns and kimono fabrics.

Kamon crests

There are thousands of Japanese family crests, and the majority of the blocks in this book were inspired by them. Designs include geometric motifs, household objects, flowers, leaves, natural phenomena and ancient aristocratic designs.

KIMONO DETAIL

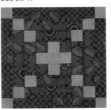
BLOCK 17

▲ **Oshima tsumugi kimono**
The subtle colours of handmade Oshima tsumugi (spun silk with a slight slubbed texture) are dyed with volcanic mud. This understated but expensive fabric is considered chic but informal. Cotton prints referencing traditional silks combine well with taupe fabrics. Some designs are suitable for interpretation in patchwork, such as block 17.

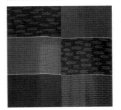
KIMONO DETAIL

BLOCK 3

▲ **Sampler juban (under-kimono)**
A man's garment made from a sample roll of Edo komon – fabric with small stencilled patterns first popularized in the Edo era; these tiny patterns exemplify the chic but understated style known as *iki*. Taupe fabrics use many similar patterns and subdued colours. The simple areas of colour inspired the design of block 3.

◀ **Kamon**
Selection of kamon designs and the blocks inspired by them. From far left: blocks 61, 65, 93, 109 and 112.

About this book

You will find a complete illustrated list of blocks on pages 34–35, showing all the blocks together. Use this to find the blocks you like, as the starting point for your quilt or project design.

Techniques and templates

The techniques section has detailed information on equipment and techniques, including photographs showing how to construct the blocks. There is also information on how to finish your quilt, from putting the blocks together to basic quilting and binding. The templates section contains all of the templates required to make the blocks.

◄ Step-by-steps
All of the techniques required to make the blocks are explained step-by-step.

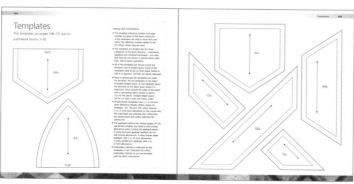

► Templates
Templates are provided for all blocks that require them. They are shown full size, so you can simply trace or photocopy them.

Block size

All of the blocks are 9 in. (22.9 cm) square at their finished size, when they are sewn together to make a quilt top or other patchwork. The actual size of each block is 9½ in. (24 cm), including seam allowances. Take care with your seam allowances when piecing narrow strips or small patches, so that all the blocks measure the same when finished. Taking fractionally larger seam allowances on blocks with many pieces (such as blocks 33 and 40) will gradually reduce the size of the block. If some of your finished blocks are too small because of larger seam allowances, try adding a border to make them fit.

Block symbols

Every block design has at-a-glance symbols indicating skill level required and technique used.

SKILL LEVEL

 EASY

 INTERMEDIATE

 ADVANCED

TECHNIQUE

 PATCHWORK

 APPLIQUÉ

Note: The patchwork and appliqué symbols together indicate that the block is made using a combination of both techniques.

Block directory

This main part of the book contains all the cutting and construction information for each block, with a photograph, fabric selection, cutting list, construction method and at-a-glance symbols giving more information. Follow either imperial or metric measurements throughout – do not switch between the two. Remember that the patchwork cutting list specifications include ¼ in. (6 mm) seam allowances.

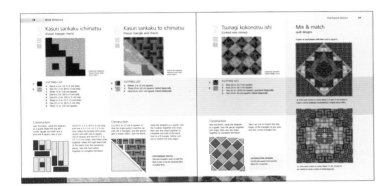

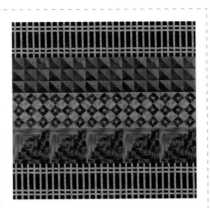

◄ **Mix-and-match quilt designs**
Each mix-and-match design idea is accompanied by a list of the blocks used to make it.

Mixing and matching blocks

All of the blocks can be mixed and matched in any combination you choose – here, for example, blocks 8, 14, 29 and 33 are combined in rows. Sampler quilts, where every block is different, are popular in Japan. Many blocks will tessellate to make all-over patterns. Use the mix-and-match ideas provided in the block directory to help plan your quilt designs and projects, changing blocks as you wish. There is also a selection of small projects in the directory, and you can use any of the blocks for these. Enjoy combining the blocks in your own way to make a unique Japanese taupe quilt.

▲ **Patchwork diagrams**
The patchwork diagrams show the order in which you should piece the patches together.

▶ **Appliqué diagrams**
The appliqué diagrams feature blue guidelines to show how to arrange the pieces of the block. Embroidery stitching is shown in red.

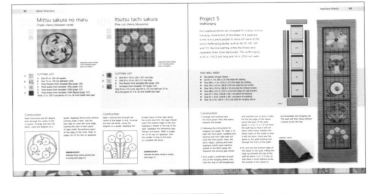

▲ **Projects**
You can use the blocks to make items other than quilts, so the projects include a cushion, table runner, wallhanging and bags as well as a lap quilt.

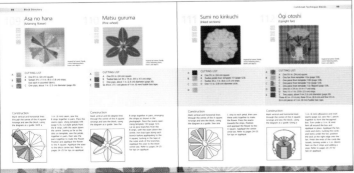

◄ **Combined technique diagrams**
Blocks constructed using both patchwork and appliqué techniques indicate how to put the patchwork pieces together (in colour), plus how to arrange the appliqué pieces using blue guidelines where appropriate. Embroidery stitching is shown in red.

Materials, Tools and Techniques

In this chapter you will find all you need to get started, from choosing fabrics and colours to all the techniques needed to make the blocks. There is advice on getting the most from different textiles, and other design tips throughout. An overview of equipment will help you gather together all you need. Finally, there are techniques and tips on completing your project.

Fabric

It all begins with the fabrics – small and large prints, shaded ombré effects, woven plaids, stripes and textures – in softly muted colours. Mastering the use of these calm, toned-down fabrics is the key to creating gorgeous contemporary quilts that combine tradition with modern style. Use the following pages to help you select the right fabrics to get that fabulous taupe look.

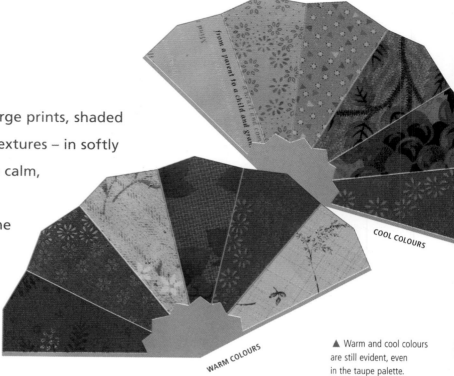

COOL COLOURS

WARM COLOURS

▲ Warm and cool colours are still evident, even in the taupe palette.

Exploring taupes

Selecting the right fabrics is your first step to creating a quilt in the Japanese taupe style. Compared with other quilting fabrics you may have used, taupes give a quilt a quiet, restful appearance. Several fabric manufacturers produce entire taupe ranges, but with a little careful selection, you will be able to include fabrics from other ranges, too.

Fabric variety adds visual interest to a quilt, especially if only one or two block patterns are being used, and taupe quilts usually include many fabrics rather than only half a dozen.

Colour

While taupe quilts may appear brown overall, on closer examination a lot of colours may be included. There are no bright pure colours (also known as 'hues'), and no bright primary or secondary colours. Darker fabrics have black added to the basic colour to make 'shades', while paler fabric colours have white added to make 'tints'. The base colour is always a tone – even base colours all have some grey added to calm them down initially. Stay away from bright and saturated ('intense') colours – save those for a different quilt.

Temperature

Taupe quilts often appear to be monochrome, because there are so many neutral fabrics included. However, even grey tones can include both warm and cool colours, and few taupe fabrics are

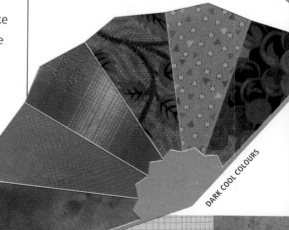

DARK COOL COLOURS

true greys, made from only black and white. Warm and cool fabrics can be included in the same quilt, with the warm fabrics making the cooler ones more attractive and vice versa. The overall temperature should appear cooler than typical American country-style quilts, with their warmer browns, although many 'country fabrics' can be used successfully alongside taupes.

Value and contrast

Conventional thinking on patchwork and appliqué often emphasizes high contrasts, so the patterns stand out well, with very light- and dark-value fabrics used together. Quilters working with

MEDIUM VALUES

LIGHT VALUES

DARK VALUES

▲ Quilters working with taupes tend to use fabrics with a similar value, although lighter or darker values can be added to create contrast or add highlights.

taupe fabrics use lower value contrasts. Definition in the patchwork or appliqué design can still be achieved by careful choice of warm or cool colours, or by varying the fabric pattern. Quilts are often predominantly dark or light. Dark and light fabrics may still be used in the same quilt, but solid black and white are not included. You may find you prefer to work with predominantly dark colours or light colours.

Red, yellow and black

Solid bright red, yellow and black – and vivid colours generally – do not appear in the taupe palette. Reds and yellows with a hint of grey may be included, such as dull brick reds and brownish yellow

ochres. Use these fabrics sparingly, such as for the centre of flowers, bias tape appliqués or block accents. If reds and yellows are too bright, they will look wrong. Some colourful prints have black backgrounds and can be incorporated into dark taupe quilts.

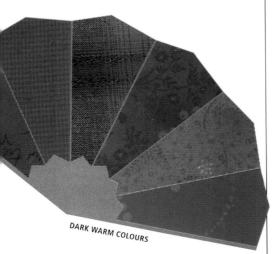

DARK WARM COLOURS

▲ Darker colours are called 'shades', with black added to them. Lighter 'tints' can be made from the same base colour, with white added instead.

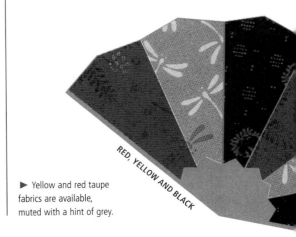

RED, YELLOW AND BLACK

► Yellow and red taupe fabrics are available, muted with a hint of grey.

Special effects

Certain fabric motifs and special woven effects are hallmarks of many Japanese fabric ranges, and taupes are no exception. Many of the woven fabrics and prints show the influence of kimono fabrics, both traditional designs and mid-20th-century fashions, while others include whimsical retro Western motifs and text. Be bold and mix florals with geometrics, prints and weaves, just as Japanese quilters do.

Printed patterns and motifs

Quilting cottons for Japanese taupe ranges include many typical designs. You may find similar fabrics and coordinates in other patchwork ranges, so look out for fabrics that continue the taupe themes and colours.

Woven patterns

Stripes, plaids and other woven designs form an integral part of many Japanese fabric collections. Some are quite thick and therefore unsuitable for fine piecing, so use them for simple piecing and as appliqué backgrounds. Using weaves off-grain adds movement. Fabrics are also printed to imitate various kinds of traditional Japanese weaves.

▶ **Kimono fabrics**
These taupe kimono fabrics are, from left: purple/ochre slubbed weave; yellow ochre with wavy lines; light grey rectangular plaid; textured straw-coloured weave; dyed khaki dots; purple/ochre slubbed weave (second detail).

▶ **Showa-era kimono**
Many taupe fabrics are similar to Showa-era (mid-20th-century) informal kimono. These patterns have a very nostalgic feeling for Japanese quilters, who can recall their mothers or grandmothers wearing kimono as everyday clothing.

Blocks using printed patterns and motifs

◄ Shaded effects (block 103)

Mottled backgrounds and motifs that appear to fade in and out, with subtle shading, show a feature known as *bokashi*, a shaded effect often seen on kimono fabric. These are especially versatile for appliqué, and can be fussy cut to add interest to petals, leaves and other pieces.

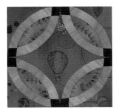

◄ Western motifs (block 64)

Retro or vintage motifs, such as antique stamps, tickets, newsprint and luggage labels, are often collaged together. Quirky nostalgic motifs like little houses, sewing notions or even hot-air balloons can also be found.

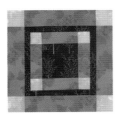

◄ Motifs from nature (block 15)

Trees and flowers are popular motifs, sometimes depicted as nature sketches or landscapes. They may be realistic or more stylized. You may want to use landscape fabrics the right way up in your blocks.

◄ Geometric and abstract designs (block 123)

All kinds of geometric designs are used, often drawn with a whimsical irregularity. Linear designs can add a sense of movement to your design, depending on placement.

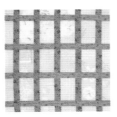

◄ Text (block 34)

Taupe fabric designers love old-fashioned script and ABC text of all descriptions. The language is often irrelevant, and may include English, French, Latin and more. Alphabetical text and words on fabric have been popular in Japan for several decades.

◄ Japanese motifs (block 68)

Traditional Japanese motifs are rarely included in taupe fabric collections from Japan, which present a Japanese view of nostalgic Western motifs. However, there are plenty of Japanese fabrics that will coordinate with taupes, so if you want to include geisha, cranes or *kanji* text, look out for similar colours – but stay away from metallic prints.

Blocks using woven patterns

◄ Stripes (block 54)

Stripes are a large part of the traditional weaver's repertoire, and may be wide or narrow. The threads are often low in contrast, so the hint of a stripe can give a very subtle sense of direction to a patchwork block or appliqué shape. Bolder stripes can create extra pattern without extra piecing.

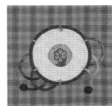

◄ Plaids and checks (block 96)

The regularity of plaids and checks make interesting backgrounds for appliqué motifs, enhancing curved patterns and calming the design. Use them off-grain to give more movement to a block.

◄ Printed stripes and plaids (block 76)

These are just like other patchwork prints, and are useful for appliqué and more detailed patchwork where a thicker genuine weave could make handling the edges difficult. Printed plaids may be at a 45-degree angle.

◄ Ombré plaid (block 95)

Woven with threads that shade in and out of colours, woven ombré plaids can give a glowing effect to an appliqué background, or add extra interest to a patchwork block.

◄ Special textures (block 81)

More complex woven patterns may be overprinted or have other fibres included for special effects. Take care when pressing special weaves that have shiny or fluffy synthetic accents. Very fancy weaves are difficult to turn under for appliqué, so keep it simple.

◄ Printed kasuri (block 18)

Traditional kasuri (a kind of ikat fabric woven from threads that are pre-dyed to create a pattern) can be very expensive and difficult to find outside Japan. Imitating fabrics like Oshima tsumugi (spun silk with a slight slubbed texture), printed kasuri makes the perfect substitute for the more delicate hand-spun and hand-woven kimono fabrics.

Equipment

If you are already a quilter, you will have most of the necessary tools for making blocks and quilts. A few handy extra items have been included here, plus some that will give your quilting experience an authentic oriental flavour.

COTON À BRODER THREAD

THREAD FOR PIECING

VARIEGATED PERLE THREAD

Scissors

Use fabric scissors for cutting fabric, embroidery scissors for cutting threads, and paper scissors for cutting paper templates. Nigiri basami (finger scissors) or 'thread snips' are sharp and easy to use for trimming threads.

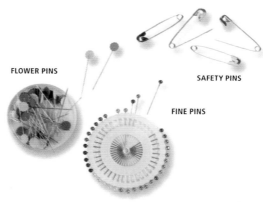

FLOWER PINS

SAFETY PINS

FINE PINS

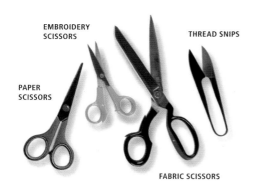

EMBROIDERY SCISSORS

THREAD SNIPS

PAPER SCISSORS

FABRIC SCISSORS

Threads

Medium thickness (50s) cotton sewing thread is best for piecing. Choose neutral colours that blend with the fabrics. Use thicker (30s or 40s) cotton thread for machine or hand quilting. Special quilting threads include variegated threads. Hand quilting threads are treated for smooth hand sewing. Other threads can be treated with beeswax or silicone wax to resist knotting – pull the thread over the edge of the wax block several times. Embroidery threads, including perle no. 12 and coton à broder, can be used for big-stitch quilting.

Pins

Select fine pins, such as good-quality dressmaking pins or 'silk pins', for piecing patchwork. 'Flower pins' have a flat head so that they do not twist on the fabric. Safety pins can be used to hold the quilt layers together for quilting, instead of tacking.

HAND SEWING NEEDLES

Erasable fabric markers

Use erasable pens and pencils to mark around templates, and to mark guidelines for appliqué and embroidered details. Always follow the manufacturer's instructions, because what removes some marks will set others permanently.

MARKING PENS

MARKING PENCILS

Needles

'Universal' needles, in size 70 or 80 (European) or 10–12 (United States), are good for machine sewing. 'Quilting' needles are sharper and best for machine quilting; try 'Microtex' for finer fabrics. Use 'sharps' or a special appliqué needle for needle-turn appliqué, where a longer needle is useful. Use crewel needles with longer eyes for embroidery. Use 'betweens' or smaller sharps for hand quilting.

MACHINE SEWING NEEDLES

MINI-
APPLIQUÉ
IRON

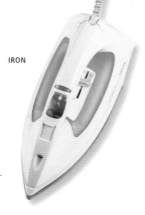

IRON

Iron and board

An ordinary iron and board is fine for pressing blocks. Use the appropriate temperature setting and avoid steaming blocks excessively, because this can distort the patchwork. A small travel iron or a mini-appliqué iron is best for ironing on bias tape. A pressing mat or small ironing board is convenient to use near your sewing matchine.

Cutting mat

A large mat is best. An A2-size mat, about 18 x 24 in. (45 x 60 cm), is a good size. Smaller mats make cutting difficult. Choose a mat with a printed grid, either imperial or metric, depending on which measuring system you prefer.

SELF-HEALING
CUTTING MAT

ERGONOMIC ROTARY CUTTER

28-MM BLADE ROTARY CUTTER

Rotary cutter

A cutter with a 28 or 45 mm blade will be most useful (blades are sold in metric sizes only). Try several cutters to find one that suits your hand best. The blades are razor sharp, so always replace the blade guard after cutting, and never leave the cutter where children or pets can reach it. The cutter must be used with a mat.

REVERSIBLE CUTTING AND PRESSING MAT

45-MM BLADE 'SQUEEZE
RELEASE' ROTARY CUTTER

RECTANGULAR QUILTING RULER

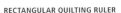

Rulers and templates

Rulers are made in many different shapes and sizes. A rectangular ruler up to about 14 in. (35 cm) long and 4½ in. (11.4 cm) wide with 60-degree and 45-degree markings is fine. A 9½ in. (24 cm) square ruler is good for squaring up finished blocks. Look at the line markings and choose colours that you will be able to see against your fabric. Use the same make of ruler whenever possible, because measurements can vary slightly between manufacturers, and between the ruler and mat – always double check before cutting. Buy a set of circle templates or make your own from template plastic. Use the appropriate size of circle template to cut circles as required for blocks. An inexpensive geometry set protractor is useful for drawing appliqué alignment markings.

Sewing machine

Useful features for patchwork and quilting include a good straight stitch and a 'needle down' option. A ¼ in. (6 mm) foot is essential for accurate patchwork. For machine quilting, a walking foot (for straight lines) and an embroidery foot (also called a quilting foot or darning foot, used for free-motion quilting) will be necessary. A large space under the machine arm will allow for easier machine quilting. An extension table will support the quilt more evenly and make machine quilting easier.

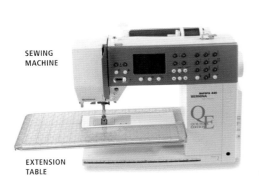

SEWING
MACHINE

EXTENSION
TABLE

¼ IN. (6 MM)
FOOT

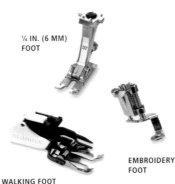

WALKING FOOT

EMBROIDERY
FOOT

SQUARE QUILTING RULER

Cutting

Rotary cutting the fabrics for your blocks whenever possible can be more accurate than using scissors. It can also be quicker, because you can cut through more than one fabric layer at a time. Some blocks require pieces to be cut from templates; use a rotary cutter whenever possible. All patchwork templates include a ¼ in. (6 mm) seam allowance. Make cutting easier by pressing the fabric smooth before you start.

Cutting safety

The rotary cutter has a very sharp blade, and it is easy to cut yourself or others accidentally, so:

- Hold the cutter firmly in the hand you write with at a 45-degree angle, and hold the ruler in place with your other hand.

- Cut with the blade against the side of the ruler – on the right if you are right-handed, and on the left if you are left-handed. The patchwork piece you are cutting is under the ruler.

- Use a sharp blade that is free from nicks and other damage. A dull blade requires more pressure when you cut, which increases the risk of the blade slipping.

- Stand up to cut if you can, and place the mat on a firm surface; a kitchen counter or sturdy table is ideal.

- Always cut away from yourself.

- Always replace the safety guard on the cutter. Make a habit of doing this after every cut.

- Wear something on your feet when you cut, in case you drop the cutter.

- Keep cutting equipment away from children and pets.

Strips

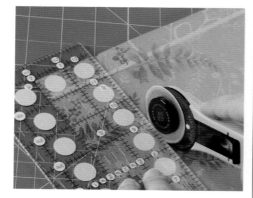

With the ruler firmly on top of the fabric, square off uneven ends of the fabric and cut off the tightly woven selvedge. Fold the fabric if required, and line up the relevant measurement on the ruler with the straight edge of the fabric. Place the rotary cutter against the ruler's edge and cut. Cut with the straight grain of the fabric whenever possible; with printed stripes and checks, cut with the pattern, unless you want an off-grain effect.

Squares and rectangles

Cut strips into squares and rectangles by aligning the ruler in the same way as before, and cutting across the strip of fabric.

Triangles

1 Cut a square in the usual way, then line up the 45-degree angle on the ruler with the edge of the square and cut along one diagonal to make a half-square triangle.

2 Cut again for quarter-square triangles.

Rotary cutting with templates

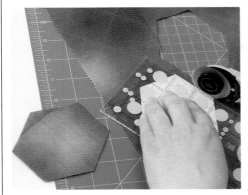

Straight-sided shapes can be cut using templates and a ruler for perfectly straight edges. Pin the template to the fabric with flat-headed or small-headed pins. Line up the ruler with the template edge and cut.

Cutting appliqué and curved pieces

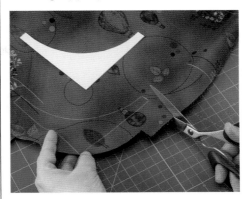

Trace or copy the relevant template and cut out. Pin the template to the fabric and draw around it with an erasable fabric marker. Cut out the piece with scissors, carefully following the drawn line.

Fussy cutting

Selecting certain areas of a print or weave for a special effect is known as fussy cutting. Look out for fabrics that can be used for these effects in your blocks.

FLORAL MOTIFS

OMBRÉ CIRCLE

▲ Stripes add a sense of direction (block 54).

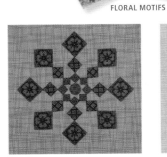

▲ Centre on individual motifs to create a pattern within the block (block 69).

▲ Use ombré fabrics to shade petals (block 80).

Piecing

Machine-sewn patchwork is relatively quick to do. Shorten the length of the machine stitch to around two-thirds the normal length – that is, around 12–14 stitches per inch (about 2–1.7 mm long). If you prefer hand piecing, draw a guideline in pencil, then sew along the guideline using very small running stitches with an occasional backstitch; start and finish with several backstitches and a knot. Use a ¼ in. (6 mm) seam allowance throughout, whichever piecing method you use. Contrasting coloured threads have been used in some photographs for clarity.

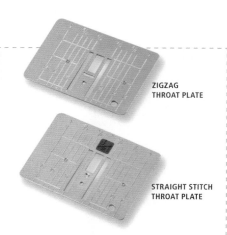

ZIGZAG THROAT PLATE

STRAIGHT STITCH THROAT PLATE

Machine stitch plates

- Replace the standard zigzag throat plate on the machine with a straight stitch plate for patchwork and quilting. The needle cannot be accidentally dragged sideways, giving a better straight stitch. Consult your machine dealer for more information.

- Remember to replace the zigzag plate afterwards, such as for overlocking or zigzagging the edges of the background squares for appliqué blocks to prevent them from fraying as you stitch the appliqué. Stitching the edges in this way is particularly useful if you are using a hand appliqué technique, where you may be handling the block a lot as you stitch. Many sewing machines have an overlock stitch, so you do not need a separate overlocker.

Laying out the block

Lay out the pieces before you begin sewing, and join them together following the individual block instructions. Some blocks have several similar-shaped pieces, so arranging the block will help you to avoid sewing pieces together in the wrong order.

Machine piecing

Place the first two pieces right sides together, making sure that the edges to be sewn line up. Align the fabric edges with the edge of the ¼ in. (6 mm) foot on the machine and sew the seam. It may help if you sit slightly to the right of the machine needle, so that you can see this easily. Use a fabric scrap as a 'leader', so that the first patchwork stitches do not get chewed up. Pin longer seams at right angles to the stitching line, and remove the pins as you sew.

▲ Stitching using a straight stitch throat plate.

▼ Overlocked edge of block.

Chain piecing

Chain piecing speeds up sewing patchwork. When you have sewn the first two pieces together, do not cut the thread. Place the next two pieces together, and sew them a stitch or two after the first two pieces. Continue in this way to make a 'chain' that can be cut up into units afterwards.

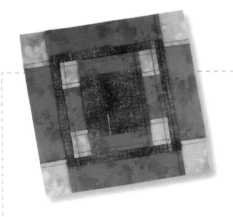

Pressing patchwork

Press each stage of the patchwork as you go along, with the seam allowance to one side; this will help stop the wadding from 'bearding' or coming through the seam later. Begin pressing from the right side of

Hand piecing (American method)

Many Japanese quilters hand piece their patchwork. The stitching lines need to be marked ¼ in. (6 mm) from the edge of each piece. Align the pieces to be sewn by pushing a pin through each end of the stitching line on the first piece. Line up the second piece underneath, right sides together, and push the pins through the ends of the line on that piece as well. With the fabrics close together, insert more pins to secure the seam for sewing. Sew seams with running stitch.

the block to avoid a 'lip' forming at the seam; you can turn it over and check the seam allowances afterwards. Press towards the darker fabric out of preference, because pressing dark towards light can cause a shadow effect on paler fabrics. Pressing in alternate directions makes the seams interlock neatly. For blocks pieced from the centre outwards, such as block 15, press seams towards the outside of the block. Press with a dry iron or just a little steam, using an up and down action so that the patchwork is not stretched and distorted – you are pressing, not ironing. Good pressing can really make a difference to your patchwork, so get it right before you continue piecing.

Triangle squares

This accurate method of making triangle squares (also called half-square triangles) avoids the necessity of sewing two bias-cut edges together, because the cut is made after the diagonal lines are sewn. Use it to make blocks like 8 and 9. An extra ⅜ in. (1 cm) seam allowance is added to the desired finished size of the square – for example, cut 4⅞ in. (12.4 cm) squares of fabric to make 4½ in. (11.4 cm) triangle squares (this extra seam allowance is included in the cutting lists for each block).

1 Draw a diagonal line on one of the squares, and place the squares together. Treat this line as the fabric edge, lining it up with the edge of the ¼ in. (6 mm) foot. Machine sew along each side of the drawn line, then cut along the line.

2 Open out both triangle squares, and press the seams towards the darker fabric. Trim the ends of the seams level with the edges of the squares.

Part-sewn seams

This arrangement of strips around a centre square copies a feature seen in Japanese architecture and flooring. Designs such as block 45 require the first seam to be only partly sewn – as little as 1 in. (2.5 cm) is enough.

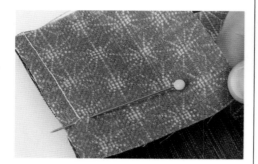

1 Assemble the outer units, as shown in the block instructions. With right sides together, line up the first two pieces. Machine sew, but only sew part of the seam, as indicated in red on the block diagram. Press the seam allowance towards the outer unit.

2 Continue to assemble the block, adding each unit in turn, but this time sewing the whole seam. Press the seam allowance towards the outside each time. When the final section has been sewn to the block, complete the first seam – the part-sewn seam – overlapping the original line of stitching slightly (the area between the pins).

3 Press the seams of the block outwards.

String patchwork

While not used as part of the blocks, string patchwork is a quick and easy way to build up the random-effect patchwork often seen in borders or sashing strips between blocks in Japanese quilts. It can also be used to make squares for alternate blocks, as shown here. The random piecing creates a lively scrap effect. Sew together long strips of scrap fabric, pressing the seams to one side. The strips can be straight or gently tapered. Cut across the strips on an angle to make squares or narrower strips, depending on the quilt design.

Inset seams

Inset seams are required when two patchwork pieces form a mitre and cannot be sewn in a straight line, such as in block 59.

1 Mark the seam allowances at the corner points with a dot and pin. Sew the first two pieces together between the dots. Start sewing by stitching back towards the dot, then sew between the dots, then reverse stitch again to finish.

2 Sew the third piece to the first piece in the same way, then sew the third piece to the second piece. Press all the seams either clockwise or anticlockwise.

Piecing curves

Designs such as block 63 use curved piecing. Straight lines are easily cut with a rotary cutter, but use scissors to cut curved pieces. Templates for the curved pieces used in the blocks are provided in the templates section at the end of the book. For circles, draw around a circle template of the appropriate size.

1 It is easier to sew curves with the convex curve below and the concave curve on top, allowing you to ease the two curves together and avoid puckers. Crease the pieces midway along the seam edge. Align the pieces at the ends and midway, and pin. Add more pins in between, easing the edges together.

2 Machine sew the seam, keeping the curves together as you go. Use a bodkin or a large pin to keep the edges together as you finish the end of the seam; otherwise, they will tend to pull apart.

Piecing a circle

Kamon crests are often traditionally used within a circle, as on the centre back of formal montsuki (crested kimono). Try using a light circle against a dark background for a similar effect. With a little practice, piecing is much quicker than appliquéing a circle as a background for kamon. It is also perfect for designs like block 120, where the bias tape ends can be hidden in the circle seam.

1 Cut out a circle from the background square, as per the block instructions. Draw balance marks around the edge like compass points – north, northeast, east and so on – on each piece. Line up the balance marks and pin these points first (green pins in photograph), with the background fabric on top. Add more pins in between, easing the edges together.

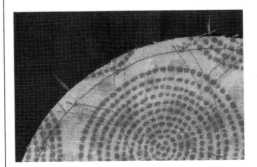

2 Machine sew the two pieces together, easing around the curve. Press the seam towards the background (outer) fabric.

Tips for piecing a circle on appliqué blocks

■ When sewing appliqué prior to inserting a circle into a background square, mark the appliqué circle on the fabric, but do not cut out the circle until the appliqué is completed. Most of the cut edge of a circle is on the bias, and will tend to stretch as the appliqué is sewn, making fitting it into the block difficult. Cutting out the circle after the appliqué is finished avoids distorting the edge. This method is preferable to machine stitching around the cut circle to stabilize it, because you need to be able to ease that edge when piecing the circle later on.

■ The same tip applies to blocks such as 114 and 123, where pieces are appliquéed to the border section of the background square before the circle centre is pieced in place – complete the appliqué, then cut out the circle from the centre.

▼ Complete the appliqué border before piecing the centre circle.

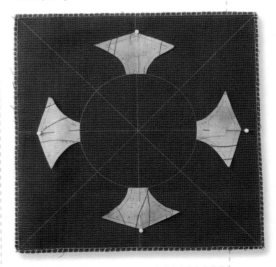

Appliqué

Appliqué is made by layering and stitching fabric pieces to a background to make a design. It is perfect for pictorial designs, such as kamon (family crests), and can be used with patchwork for more detailed blocks. Japanese quilters combine patchwork and appliqué. Appliqué can be hand or machine sewn. Fused or bonded appliqué can be edged with machine stitching.

Freezer paper appliqué

This method uses paper templates behind the fabric, which is folded and pressed over the paper edge for accuracy. Freezer paper has a waxy side that can be ironed to the back of the fabric, sticking the template in place; the waxy wrappers from copier paper can be used instead. Cut the paper templates as mirror images of the templates on pages 116–126 and without adding any extra to the edges. Cut out the fabric after ironing on the template, adding a ¼ in. (6 mm) turning allowance all around. After sewing the appliqué shape in place, cut away the background fabric behind it, leaving about a ¼ in. (6 mm) overlap, and gently pull the paper out. Alternatively, cut a slit in the background fabric to remove the paper.

Fused appliqué

This very quick appliqué method involves ironing fusible webbing to the back of the fabric, cutting out the pieces and ironing them onto a backing fabric. Like freezer paper appliqué, the appliqué templates need to be traced as mirror images onto the back of the fusible web paper. The fabric appliqué pieces need no turning allowance. The edges are best stitched with a machine satin, zigzag or blanket stitch, because the fusible webbing stiffens the fabrics, making hand sewing difficult.

CIRCLE TEMPLATES

Arranging the appliqué

Arrange the pieces, following the block instructions. Depending on the design, you will need to mark various guidelines onto the background fabric in order to align the appliqué pieces. Mark these with a pen or pencil that can be washed out or erased later. Draw 45-degree lines with diagonal lines linking the block corners, plus vertical and horizontal lines; 60-degree lines can be marked from a horizontal or vertical centre line with the relevant angle line on your quilting ruler. Use a protractor for smaller angle measurements. Mark alignment circles with circle templates.

BLOCK 75 DIAGRAM

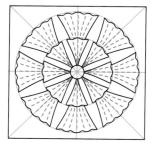

ERASABLE BLUE GUIDELINES

Needle-turn appliqué

This method gives a firm, strong and neat edge to the appliqué. All of the blocks in this book were made using this method. You will need to add an ⅛ in. (3 mm) turning allowance all around each piece, except for raw edges that are tucked under other appliqué pieces or hidden in seams. Curved appliqué shapes have mostly bias edges and the turn under is small, so it is not necessary to clip the fabric around curves; just ease it under. Only deep V shapes need clipping.

1 Tack the shape to the background with small stitches about ¼ in. (6 mm) long and exactly ¼ in. (6 mm) from the cut edge. The tacking stitches will prevent too much fabric from being turned under.

2 Use an appliqué needle or a long sharp to turn under the raw edge a little at a time as you sew. Use the point of the needle to stroke the fabric edge into place. Crease the turned edge with your fingers as you go. Start and finish sewing on a long edge, with a few knots and tiny running stitches hidden under the edge of the appliqué. Come up through the folded edge of the appliqué shape and stitch down into the backing fabric, keeping the stitches at right angles to the folded edge so that they are almost invisible.

3 Create sharp points and corners by leaving the last couple of stitches loose, pushing the point of the fabric under the shape as far as possible, and then gently tightening up the sewing thread. The loose stitches will tighten up and the point will pull out perfectly.

FUSIBLE BIAS TAPE

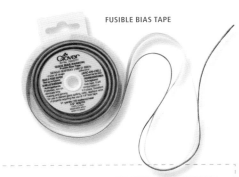

Fusible bias tape

Ready-made fusible bias tape is quick and easy to use to represent stems, cords, branches and other design elements. It is made in Japan in various colours. Select tape with more muted shades to go with taupe fabrics. Following the manufacturer's instructions, iron the bias tape in place, then sew down the edges with small stitches, as for needle-turn appliqué.

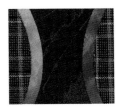

▲ Where bias tape overlaps the raw edges of appliqués, there is no need to turn under the fabric edge. Simply cover the raw edge with tape (block 66).

▲ Multicoloured bias tape is available, and looks particularly attractive when overlapped (block 97).

▲ The shading on multicoloured bias tape can give additional variety to repeated strips (block 116).

▲ Depending on the block construction, the ends of the bias tape can be sewn into patchwork seams, simply turned under or covered with appliqués (block 81).

Embellishment

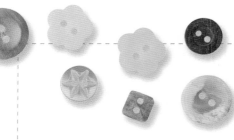

Japanese quilters often add embroidery, buttons and other embellishments, such as yoyos, to their quilt blocks, representing details such as leaf veins or tiny flowers. Embellishments are particularly useful for adding details to appliqué blocks, but you can also use them for extra interest on patchwork blocks. Sew embroidery before the blocks are sewn together and quilted, or work the stitches through the wadding and backing as quilting.

Buttons

There are many attractive buttons that may be used to embellish taupe quilts, a feature that has possibly crossed over from American country-style quilts. Look for pretty buttons in various materials and colours that will harmonize with your design. Natural materials, including wood, mother-of-pearl and other shells, look beautiful with taupe fabrics. Plastic buttons, in appropriate colours, are useful if your quilt is likely to be washed.

Yoyos

Yoyos are gathered fabric embellishments, sometimes called Suffolk puffs. They are quick and easy to make, adding a pleasing textured effect to a block design.

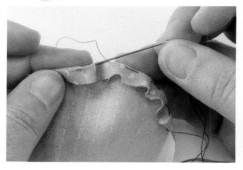

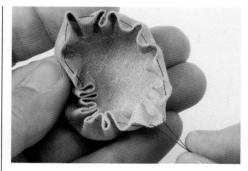

1 Cut a cardboard circle twice the required diameter of the yoyo. Cut a fabric circle of the same diameter plus ½ in. (1.3 cm). Turn under a ¼ in. (6 mm) hem all around by pressing the fabric circle around the cardboard template. Using a strong doubled thread, sew a ring of running stitch around the circle, stitching close to the folded edge. Start with a knot and leave a long tail of thread.

2 Gather up the yoyo by pulling gently on the ends of the thread. Pull up the gathers closely, making the opening as small as possible. Knot the thread ends together and stitch them out of sight. Flatten out the yoyo slightly with the gather in the centre, press lightly and appliqué to the block.

3 A yoyo maker is a handy tool for making lots of identical yoyos, and is especially useful for smaller sizes. It is not necessary to press a hem allowance before gathering. The fabric is clipped between the plastic plate and the disc, and trimmed to about ⅛ in. (3 mm) all around. Holes in the plate allow even placement of the gathering stitches. Once the stitches are in place, simply remove the fabric from the plate and disc and pull up the threads.

Embroidery stitches

Many embroidery stitches make attractive additions to the blocks. The following are all used for details on the appliqué and combined technique blocks. The back of the block will be hidden inside the quilt, so you can start and finish with a knot on the back. Other embroidery stitches, such as blanket stitch or feather stitch, may be used to edge shapes or add accents.

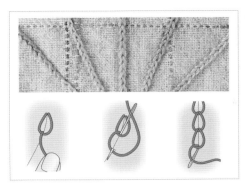

▲ **Chain stitch**

A line of chain stitch is wider than stem stitch. It is useful for creating slightly heavier lines but where bias tape would be too solid. Use the thumb of your non-sewing hand to throw a loop, take the needle back through the starting hole and take a stitch forward, coming up inside the loop. Pull the stitch closed and repeat. Secure the last loop with a small stitch.

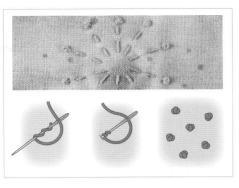

▲ **French knot**

Use French knots for flower centres and stamens. Bring the thread to the surface and, holding the needle in your sewing hand, wrap the thread around the needle twice. Keeping the thread taut so that it stays wrapped around the needle, take the needle back through the fabric near the starting point.

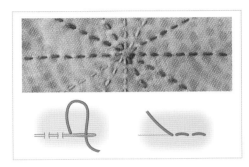

▲ **Running stitch**

Adding an accent that looks a little like traditional Japanese sashiko stitches, use running stitch for flower centres, leaf veins, and other details. It is good for a rustic, country look. Keep the stitches small and even.

► **Lazy daisy stitch**

Arrange individual chain stitches to make little flowers, clusters of blossom or other details – known as lazy daisy stitch.

Embroidery thread

Cotton perle no. 12 thickness, coton à broder and fine sashiko threads are all suitable for adding embroidered details. There are many hand-dyed and shaded threads available for an interesting effect. Select colours that harmonize with your taupe fabrics. Slightly darker, brighter or more richly coloured threads can work well with taupes, because the small amounts of stronger colour will not overpower the overall calm effect of the fabrics.

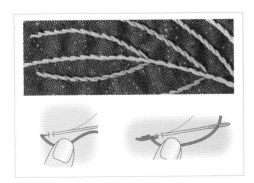

▲ **Stem stitch**

Use stem stitch for a solid but fine line. Pulling the thread out of the way below the stitching line with your non-sewing hand, take a small stitch backward towards the starting point and repeat.

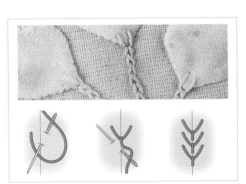

▲ **Fly stitch**

Sew an individual fly stitch where flower appliqués join a line of chain stitches. Work fly stitch like a single chain stitch, but with the starting point of the stitch open rather than closed. It can also be worked in vertical or horizontal rows, for a V-shaped pattern.

Finishing

Blocks can be arranged or 'set' in various ways for different quilt designs. Once you have decided upon the design, simply sew the blocks together in rows and then sew the rows together to complete the quilt top. The next step is to sandwich the top, wadding and backing layers. An optional border can help to frame the blocks, while hand or machine quilting holds the layers together securely.

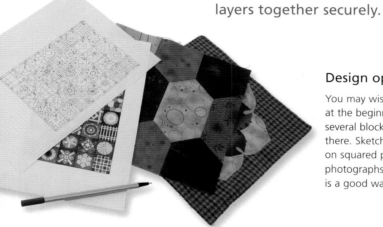

Design options

You may wish to decide the block layout at the beginning of your project, or make several blocks and take the design from there. Sketching a plan of the project on squared paper will help. Taking photographs of the finished blocks is a good way to plan a sampler quilt.

Sashing and posts

Sashing refers to strips inserted between the quilt blocks. It separates them visually as well as separating the construction seams from one block to the next. It can be a good place to introduce a touch of colour, and careful choice of sashing can help to bring a sense of unity to blocks made with different fabrics. Sashing with posts means there are smaller squares added to the sashing at the corners of the blocks, with all the sashing strips measuring the same length as the block sides.

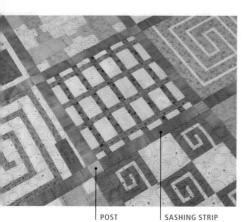

POST   SASHING STRIP

Sampler quilts

- Using just one of each block in a quilt is called a sampler. The blocks can be sewn straight together, which usually works best if you have been very colour coordinated with the blocks – almost inevitable with the calm, coordinated taupe fabrics, where one fabric seems to go with almost any other.
- Alternating between patchwork and appliqué blocks is a successful arrangement, because there are no seams that need to match between one block and the next.
- Alternating a variety of blocks with just one pieced design produces a chequerboard effect.
- Alternating a variety of blocks with plain squares makes more complicated blocks cover a larger area. Plain blocks are a good place to show off more elaborate quilting designs or a large-scale print that you do not want to cut up too small.

CHEQUERBOARD SAMPLER

Adding a quilt border

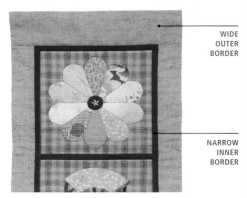

WIDE OUTER BORDER

NARROW INNER BORDER

To add a simple border, measure the patchwork vertically through the centre, and cut two border pieces to that length. Pin the borders to the sides of the patchwork, lining up the ends and the centre, and then ease the side of the patchwork to the border. Sew, and press the seams towards the border strips. Repeat this process for the top and bottom border pieces. Measuring through the centre each time is more accurate than measuring along the patchwork edge. A series of narrow and wide borders can be added in the same way. Quilt borders can be whatever width you like, and blocks can be bordered individually, too. The border can also be made from patchwork, with a narrow inner border between it and the blocks. The border used for the lap quilt project (page 61) uses the part-sewn seam method (page 22), so the border seems to spin around the quilt.

Making the quilt sandwich

The backing fabric and wadding should be about 2 in. (5 cm) larger than the quilt top all around. If the backing is pieced, use a ½ in. (1.3 cm) seam and press the seams open. Press the fabrics and smooth out the backing on a flat, clean surface, covering any important tabletops with heavy cardboard or wooden sheeting. Hold the backing edges down at intervals with masking tape. Spread the wadding on top and smooth out. Repeat with the quilt top, making sure that the corners are square. Starting at the centre, tack the layers together. You may wish to pin the layers with dressmaking pins, or omit the hand tacking and tack with safety pins instead. Japanese quilters often tack the layers with a diagonal stitch, holding the layers very securely, rather than straight tacking. Using a teaspoon to lever up the point of the needle after each stitch prevents your fingers from getting sore.

On-point settings

Many blocks work well set on a 45-degree angle. It can make the overall design of the quilt more lively and add interest to the blocks. If you plan to use appliqué blocks on point, you may need to rotate the motif on the block by 45-degrees, so that it still looks balanced. The blocks are still sewn together in rows, but diagonally, with a half- or quarter-block triangle at each end. The lap quilt project turns blocks on point and separates them with a chequerboard of unpieced squares of woven plaid. The chrysanthemum quilting pattern on the plaid squares was adapted from block 108. For the measurements for the side and corner triangles, see the project instructions on page 61.

LAP QUILT

Wadding

Choose an appropriate wadding for your quilting technique (your quilt store will be able to advise you). Puffy polyester waddings give dimension to appliqué blocks, but cotton and cotton/polyester blends are better for machine quilting.

NATURAL COTTON WADDING

BLACK BLENDED WADDING

BLEACHED COTTON WADDING

Hand quilting

1 Many Japanese quilters work without a quilting frame, because the diagonal tacking method holds the layers securely, but you can use a frame if you prefer. Begin quilting from the centre. Quilting 'in the ditch' along seam lines between blocks is a good starting point; quilt block details later. Use thread slightly darker than the fabric.

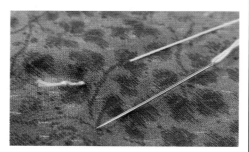

2 To hand quilt, start by tying two small knots at the end of the quilting thread. From the front of the quilt, take a long stitch in the opposite direction to the way you will quilt, 'popping' the two knots through the fabric and wadding. With your non-sewing hand under the quilt, take small running stitches in a rocking motion, going through all the layers. Feel the needle point emerging under the quilt and immediately push the point up again, taking several stitches before pulling the needle through. Using a thimble on each index finger will protect them. When the thread is finished, turn the quilt over and tie two more knots, popping these through the backing and into the quilt.

Machine quilting

Machine quilting is less popular than hand quilting in Japan, but equally popular in the West. It has a stronger linear effect than hand quilting. Start and finish at the edge of the piece if you can, to avoid needing to sew in the thread ends afterwards. Continuous-line patterns are easiest to quilt.

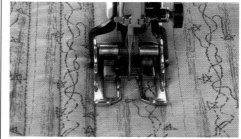

1 Use a walking foot on the machine to feed the layers of the quilt sandwich through at the same rate, in order to prevent puckering. Use it for quilting straight lines, in the ditch or with a small gap around motifs, and for grids, parallel lines and gentle curves. With a zigzag throat plate on the machine, you can quilt any embroidery stitches your machine has installed.

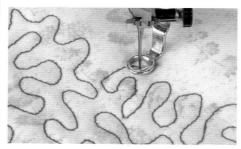

2 Free-motion quilting requires an embroidery, quilting or darning foot. With the machine feed dogs set in the down position, guide the quilt through the machine, moving the quilt in any direction, but evenly to maintain a consistent stitch length.

Machine quilting designs

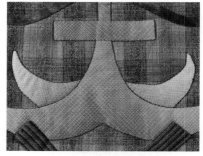

▲ Stitch around the edges of appliqué motifs to add definition.

▲ Contour quilting leaves a small space between the appliqué and the stitching.

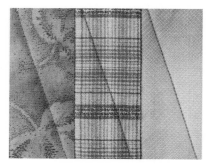

▲ Diagonal lines and quilting in the ditch keep the stitching continuous.

Big-stitch quilting and tying

Giving a similar effect to traditional Japanese sashiko, big-stitch quilting uses thicker thread and is intended to be seen. Using buttons to tie the layers of the quilt together at intervals provides additional embellishment.

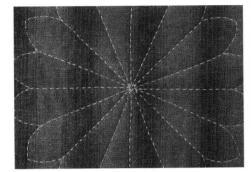

1 Use it to add decorative quilting designs to the quilt. Threads like perle no. 12, fine sashiko thread and coton à broder are all suitable.

2 Buttons may also be used to tie the quilt at intervals, stitching through each button individually several times, right through the quilt layers.

Binding

The quilt can be bound with strips cut from coordinating fabric. These can be cut on the straight grain or on the bias. If you need to join strips for binding, press the joining seams open to reduce bulk and consider joining with a mitred seam. Trim the backing and wadding to match the edge of the quilt top. Tack or sew all around the top, close to the edge, to hold the layers together while applying the binding. Cut 1½ in. (3.8 cm) wide binding strips, to the same length as the first edge to be bound and two 2 in. (5 cm) longer than the remaining edges. Pin the first two strips to the corresponding quilt edges along the front of the quilt, setting the strip edge approximately ¼ in. (6 mm) away from the quilt edge, and sew. Fold the binding around the edge, turn under a ¼ in. (6 mm) allowance, and hem by hand with small stitches to the back of the quilt. Repeat for the two remaining edges, but allow the binding to overlap by 1 in. (2.5 cm) at each end when machine sewing. Fold and sew in these ends before hemming the binding to the back of the quilt.

▶ **Scrap blocks**
Piece scraps together and then trim them to form random blocks or strips for sashing and borders.

Irregular designs

■ Japanese quilt blocks are often combined in irregular layouts, with borders of varying sizes added to the different blocks. The table runner (page 79) offsets the blocks by adding strips of patchwork to alternate sides, giving an asymmetric layout.

■ Smaller blocks and sections of pieced squares, rectangles, triangles or random string patchwork may be included in your designs. The smaller units used to make blocks like 8 or 13 can be used separately as smaller blocks.

■ Visually simpler appliqué blocks such as 71 and circular flower designs like 106 can be appliquéed over simple patchwork or across joined blocks.

■ A one-of-a-kind quilt needs planning to achieve an apparently random effect. Making a number of blocks and laying pieces out in various ways can be a good starting point if you like to work intuitively, adding pieces and squaring up patchwork as you go.

■ Scraps left over from piecing the blocks can be sewn together at random, working from the centre outwards, and then cut to size. You will need to do a lot of trimming and adding pieces if you work this way. Alternatively, plan out your unique quilt on graph paper first.

Block Directory

The directory contains photographs, instructions and construction diagrams for making all 125 Japanese taupe quilt blocks. The directory is divided into patchwork and appliqué blocks, plus blocks that combine both techniques. The degree of difficulty is indicated for each block, so you can begin with those that suit your patchwork or appliqué skills, tackling more challenging blocks later. All of the blocks can be mixed and matched to create your own unique projects. You can adapt the mix-and-match ideas suggested in the directory, or make one of the six projects using your favourite collection of blocks.

Choosing blocks

All 125 blocks are shown together here; use this as an at-a-glance resource to compare and choose blocks. If you prefer stronger or brighter colours in your quilts, it is easy to change the fabrics to suit your quilt style.

Block categories

The blocks have been created using the most appropriate (and easiest) technique for the design.

Patchwork blocks (1–65)
These are geometric blocks inspired by kamon (family crests), kasuri (ikat) woven fabrics and other traditional patterns. Some blocks include triangles, wedges and curved pieces. Templates are provided for more complex shapes. The light, medium and dark tones used for the patchwork blocks make it easy to change the fabrics to suit your own taste.

Appliqué blocks (66–105)
Pictorial designs, including many kamon, are most easily created in appliqué. All of the appliqué blocks in this book were made using the needle-turn method, but other appliqué techniques can be used if you prefer. Embroidery, bias tape or embellishment is sometimes used to add details. More colourful taupe fabrics are used for the appliqué blocks, often in a naturalistic way, but you can recolour the blocks to suit your project.

Combined technique blocks (106–125)
Some of the block designs are most easily made by using both patchwork and appliqué. Pieces are patchworked together before being appliquéed to the background fabric, and pieced circular kamon crests are neatly inserted into the block border.

Patchwork blocks

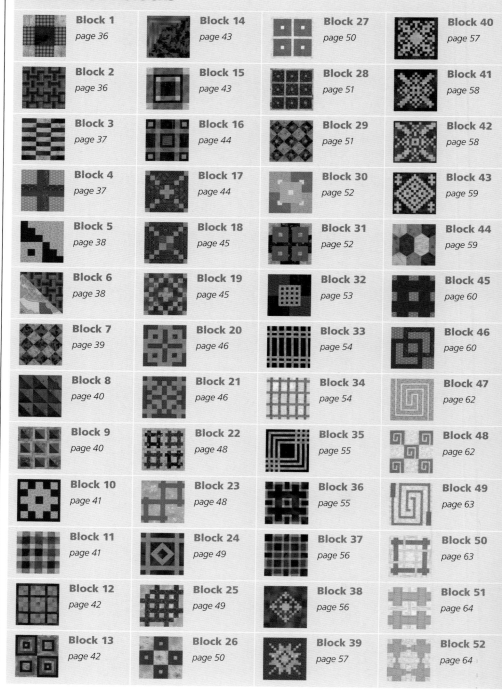

Block 1 — page 36
Block 2 — page 36
Block 3 — page 37
Block 4 — page 37
Block 5 — page 38
Block 6 — page 38
Block 7 — page 39
Block 8 — page 40
Block 9 — page 40
Block 10 — page 41
Block 11 — page 41
Block 12 — page 42
Block 13 — page 42

Block 14 — page 43
Block 15 — page 43
Block 16 — page 44
Block 17 — page 44
Block 18 — page 45
Block 19 — page 45
Block 20 — page 46
Block 21 — page 46
Block 22 — page 48
Block 23 — page 48
Block 24 — page 49
Block 25 — page 49
Block 26 — page 50

Block 27 — page 50
Block 28 — page 51
Block 29 — page 51
Block 30 — page 52
Block 31 — page 52
Block 32 — page 53
Block 33 — page 54
Block 34 — page 54
Block 35 — page 55
Block 36 — page 55
Block 37 — page 56
Block 38 — page 56
Block 39 — page 57

Block 40 — page 57
Block 41 — page 58
Block 42 — page 58
Block 43 — page 59
Block 44 — page 59
Block 45 — page 60
Block 46 — page 60
Block 47 — page 62
Block 48 — page 62
Block 49 — page 63
Block 50 — page 63
Block 51 — page 64
Block 52 — page 64

Appliqué blocks

Block 53
page 65

Block 54
page 65

Block 55
page 66

Block 56
page 66

Block 57
page 67

Block 58
page 68

Block 59
page 68

Block 60
page 69

Block 61
page 69

Block 62
page 70

Block 63
page 70

Block 64
page 71

Block 65
page 71

Block 66
page 72

Block 67
page 72

Block 68
page 74

Block 69
page 74

Block 70
page 75

Block 71
page 75

Block 72
page 76

Block 73
page 76

Block 74
page 77

Block 75
page 77

Block 76
page 78

Block 77
page 78

Block 78
page 80

Block 79
page 80

Block 80
page 81

Block 81
page 81

Block 82
page 82

Block 83
page 82

Block 84
page 83

Block 85
page 84

Block 86
page 84

Block 87
page 85

Block 88
page 85

Block 89
page 86

Block 90
page 86

Block 91
page 87

Block 92
page 87

Block 93
page 88

Block 94
page 88

Block 95
page 89

Block 96
page 90

Block 97
page 90

Block 98
page 91

Block 99
page 91

Block 100
page 92

Block 101
page 92

Block 102
page 94

Block 103
page 94

Block 104
page 95

Block 105
page 95

Combined technique blocks

Block 106
page 96

Block 107
page 96

Block 108
page 97

Block 109
page 98

Block 110
page 98

Block 111
page 99

Block 112
page 99

Block 113
page 100

Block 114
page 100

Block 115
page 102

Block 116
page 102

Block 117
page 103

Block 118
page 103

Block 119
page 104

Block 120
page 104

Block 121
page 105

Block 122
page 105

Block 123
page 106

Block 124
page 106

Block 125
page 107

1 Kasuri koshi kaku
(Kasuri square check)

Inspired by traditional
Japanese kasuri (ikat)
woven fabrics.

		CUTTING LIST
A		A One 4½ in. (11.4 cm) square.
B		B Four 4½ x 3 in. (11.4 x 7.6 cm) strips.
C		C Four 3 in. (7.6 cm) squares.

Construction
Sew the block, using the diagram
as a guide. Sew the pieces together
into strips, then sew the strips
together to complete the block.

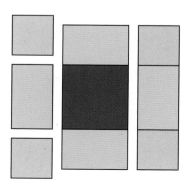

2 Shima ichimatsu
(Stripe check)

Inspired by traditional
Japanese patterns and
woven kimono fabrics.

		CUTTING LIST
A		A Thirty-six 2 in. (5 cm) squares.

Construction
Cut the squares in groups of three,
so that each set of three squares
has a matching stripe pattern. Sew
the block, using the diagram as a
guide. Arrange the patches so
that the stripes appear to weave
together. Sew the pieces together
into strips, then sew the strips
together to complete the block.

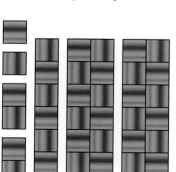

ALTERNATIVE DESIGN
Cut eighteen dark and eighteen
light squares, and arrange as a
classic chequerboard.

3 Sakiori shima
(Rag-weave stripe)

Inspired by sakiori rag-weave rugs.

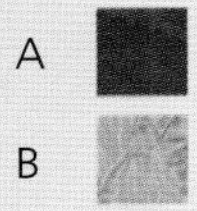

		CUTTING LIST
A		A Fourteen 3½ x 1½ in. (8.9 x 3.8 cm) strips.
B		B Thirteen 3½ x 1½ in. (8.9 x 3.8 cm) strips.

Construction

Sew the block, using the diagram as a guide. Alternate the position of light and dark fabrics. Sew the pieces together into strips, then sew the strips together to complete the block.

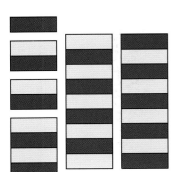

ALTERNATIVE DESIGN
Reverse the position of light and dark pieces in adjacent blocks, or use assorted fabrics for A or B.

4 Yotsu kumi sujikai
(Four paired braces)

Inspired by geometric kamon (family crests).

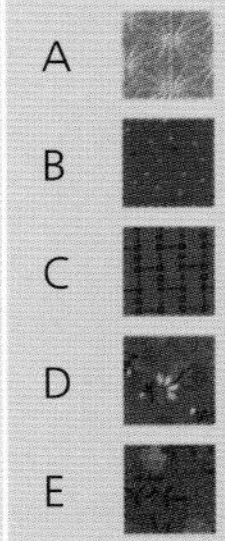

		CUTTING LIST
A		A Four 3¾ in. (9.5 cm) squares.
B		B One 5 x 1¾ in. (12.7 x 4.4 cm) strip.
		B One 3¾ x 1¾ in. (9.5 x 4.4 cm) strip.
C		C One 5 x 1¾ in. (12.7 x 4.4 cm) strip.
		C One 3¾ x 1¾ in. (9.5 x 4.4 cm) strip.
D		D One 5 x 1¾ in. (12.7 x 4.4 cm) strip.
		D One 3¾ x 1¾ in. (9.5 x 4.4 cm) strip.
E		E One 5 x 1¾ in. (12.7 x 4.4 cm) strip.
		E One 3¾ x 1¾ in. (9.5 x 4.4 cm) strip.

Construction

Sew the block, using the diagram as a guide. Arrange the four strip fabrics to make a woven effect. If using a directional or scenic fabric for the squares, make sure that each is the right way up. Sew the shorter strip to each square first, then sew the longer strip. Sew these units together in pairs, then sew together to complete the block.

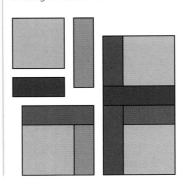

5 Kasuri sankaku ichimatsu
(Kasuri triangle check)

Inspired by traditional Japanese kasuri (ikat) woven fabrics.

CUTTING LIST

A
B

A	Two 5 x 2 in. (12.7 x 5 cm) strips.
A	Two 3½ x 2 in. (8.9 x 5 cm) strips.
A	Three 1½ in. (3.8 cm) squares.
B	One 8 x 2 in. (20.3 x 5 cm) strip.
B	One 6½ x 2 in. (16.5 x 5 cm) strip.
B	Three 5 x 2 in. (12.7 x 5 cm) strips.
B	One 3½ x 2 in. (8.9 x 5 cm) strip.
B	Three 1½ in. (3.8 cm) squares.

6 Kasuri sankaku to ichimatsu
(Kasuri triangle and check)

Inspired by traditional Japanese kasuri (ikat) woven fabrics.

CUTTING LIST

A
B

A	Fifteen 2 in. (5 cm) squares.
A	Three 2⅜ in. (6 cm) squares, halved diagonally.
B	One 9⅞ in. (25.1 cm) square, halved diagonally.

Construction

Sew the block, using the diagram as a guide. Make the top left corner square unit with one A and one B square, one A and one B 3½ x 2 in. (8.9 x 5 cm) strip, and one A 5 x 2 in. (12.7 x 5 cm) strip. Make the bottom left corner square unit with one A square, two B squares and two B 5 x 2 in. (12.7 x 5 cm) strips. Sew these units together. Make the right-hand half of the block from the remaining pieces. Sew the two halves together to complete the block.

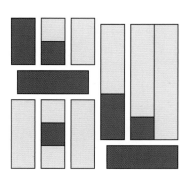

Construction

Cut the 2 in. (5 cm) A squares so that the stripe pattern matches up with the A triangles, and the pieces give a woven effect. Sew the block, using the diagram as a guide. Sew the A pieces together into strips, then sew the strips together to complete one half of the block. Sew to a B triangle, taking care not to stretch the bias edges.

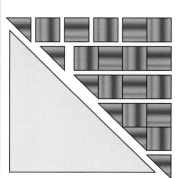

PATCHWORK NOTES

Only one B triangle is used, so make this block in pairs or use the remaining fabric in another block.

7 Tsunagi kokonotsu ishi
(Linked nine stones)

Inspired by geometric kamon (family crests).

CUTTING LIST

A   Nine 2⅝ in. (6.7 cm) squares.
B   Four 2⅝ in. (6.7 cm) squares.
B   One 4¼ in. (10.8 cm) squares, quartered diagonally.
B   Four 2⅜ in. (6 cm) squares, halved diagonally.

Construction

Sew the block, using the diagram as a guide. Sew the pieces together into strips, then sew the strips together to complete the block.

Take care not to stretch the bias edges of the triangles as you sew. Sew the corner triangles last.

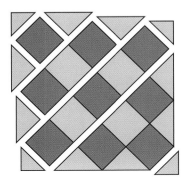

ALTERNATIVE DESIGN
Cut the dark squares from assorted fabrics for a scrap look.

Mix & match
quilt designs

Frames or medallions with four central squares

▲ From outer corners to centre, blocks 2, 6 and 14 are rotated to create a central arabesque surrounded by a striped weave effect.

▲ From outer corners to centre, blocks 13, 46, 23 and 25 are rotated to create a series of linked diagonals.

8 Uroko
(Scales)

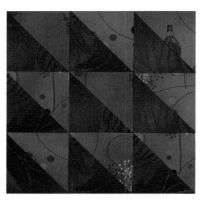

Inspired by geometric kamon (family crests).

 A
 B

CUTTING LIST

A   Five 3⅞ in. (9.8 cm) squares.

B   Five 3⅞ in. (9.8 cm) squares.

9 Kawari masu
(Stacking boxes variation)

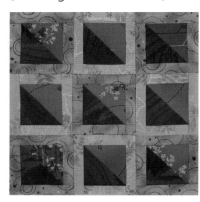

Inspired by geometric kamon (family crests).

A

B

C

D

CUTTING LIST

A   Five 2⅞ in. (7.3 cm) squares.

B   Five 2⅞ in. (7.3 cm) squares.

C   Ten 3½ x 1 in. (8.9 x 2.5 cm) strips.

C   Ten 2½ x 1 in. (6.4 x 2.5 cm) strips.

D   Eight 3½ x 1 in. (8.9 x 2.5 cm) strips.

D   Eight 2½ x 1 in. (6.4 x 2.5 cm) strips.

Construction

Make ten triangle square units, using one A and one B square for each pair of units (page 21). Sew the block, using the diagram as a guide. Sew nine triangle square units together into strips of three, then sew the strips together to complete the block.

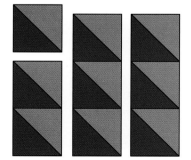

PATCHWORK NOTES

Keep the leftover half-square triangle unit for another block, or make this block in pairs using nine squares of each fabric.

Construction

Make ten triangle square units, using one A and one B square for each pair of units (page 21). Sew the block, using the diagram as a guide. Sew the short border strips to each triangle square unit, then add the longer strips. Sew units together into strips of three, then sew the strips together to complete the block.

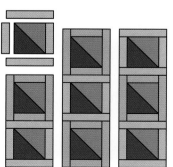

PATCHWORK NOTES

Keep the leftover triangle square unit for another block, or make this block in pairs using nine squares each of A and B fabric.

10 Kasuri kawari hana
(Kasuri flower variation)

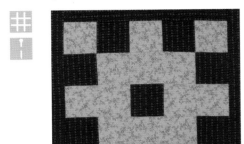

Inspired by traditional Japanese kasuri (ikat) woven fabrics.

CUTTING LIST

A
B

A   Two 9½ x 1¼ in. (24 x 3.2 cm) strips.
A   Two 8 x 1¼ in. (20.3 x 3.2 cm) strips.
A   Nine 2 in. (5 cm) squares.
B   Two 2 x 5 in. (5 x 12.7 cm) strips.
B   Two 3½ x 2 in. (8.9 x 5 cm) strips.
B   Six 2 in. (5 cm) squares.

Construction

Sew the block, using the diagram as a guide. Sew the pieces together into strips, then sew the strips together and add the border to complete the block.

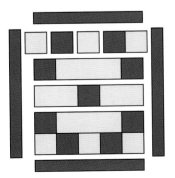

11 Kasuri koshi
(Kasuri check)

Inspired by traditional Japanese kasuri (ikat) woven fabrics.

CUTTING LIST

A
B
C

A   Nine 2 in. (5 cm) squares.
B   Twelve 2 x 1¾ in. (5 x 4.4 cm) strips.
B   Twelve 2 x 1½ in. (5 x 3.8 cm) strips.
C   Eight 1¾ x 1½ in. (4.4 x 3.8 cm) strips.
C   Four 1¾ in. (4.4 cm) squares.
C   Four 1½ in. (3.8 cm) squares.

Construction

Sew the block, using the diagram as a guide. Sew the pieces together into strips, then sew the strips together to complete the block.

Note that the four larger C squares go at the corners of the block; the four smaller C squares go in the centre area.

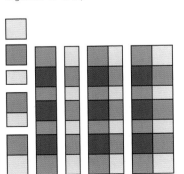

ALTERNATIVE DESIGN
Cut the A squares from assorted fabrics for a scrap look.

12 Atsuita koshi
(Noh robe check)

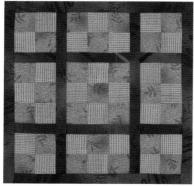

Inspired by antique Noh robe costume.

CUTTING LIST

A
B
C

- A Two 9½ x 1 in. (24 x 2.5 cm) strips.
- A Four 8½ x 1 in. (21.6 x 2.5 cm) strips.
- A Two 3½ x 1 in. (8.9 x 2.5 cm) strips.
- A Four 2½ x 1 in. (6.4 x 2.5 cm) strips.
- B Twenty-five 1½ in. (3.8 cm) squares.
- C Twenty-four 1½ in. (3.8 cm) squares.

Construction

Sew the block, using the diagram as a guide. Sew the squares together into units, then sew the units together with the sashing strips. Add the border to complete the block.

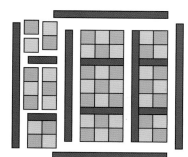

ALTERNATIVE DESIGN
Cut the B squares from assorted fabrics for a scrap look.

13 Yottsu masu
(Four square measures)

Inspired by geometric kamon (family crests).

CUTTING LIST

A
B
C
D

- A Four 5 x 1 in. (12.7 x 2.5 cm) strips.
- A Four 4 x 1 in. (10.2 x 2.5 cm) strips.
- A Four 3 x 1 in. (7.6 x 2.5 cm) strips.
- A Eight 2 x 1 in. (5 x 2.5 cm) strips.
- A Four 1 in. (2.5 cm) squares.
- B Cut all of the above again in this fabric.
- C Eight 4 x 1 in. (10.2 x 2.5 cm) strips.
- C Eight 3 x 1 in. (7.6 x 2.5 cm) strips.
- D Four 1 in. (2.5 cm) squares.

Construction

Sew the block, using the diagram as a guide. Sew each quarter of the block separately, starting at the centre of each unit and sewing the strips in sequence, then sew the four quarter units together. Take care to keep the ¼ in. (6 mm) seam allowances accurate when sewing so many narrow strips.

14 Marutagoya
(Round log cabin)

This popular patchwork design can be combined to make a very large seigaiha (wave) pattern.

 A

B

CUTTING LIST

A   One 1½ in. (3.8 cm) strip in these lengths: 9, 8, 7½, 6½, 6, 5, 4½, 3½, 3 and 2 in. (22.9, 20.3, 19, 16.5, 15.2, 12.7, 11.4, 8.9, 7.6 and 5 cm).

A   One 1½ in. (3.8. cm) square.

B   One 1 in. (2.5 cm) strip in these lengths: 9½, 9, 8, 7½, 6½, 6, 5, 4½, 3½, 3, 2 and 1½ in. (24, 22.9, 20.3, 19, 16.5, 15.2, 12.7, 11.4, 8.9, 7.6, 5 and 3.8 cm).

Construction

Sew the block, using the diagram as a guide. Working from the centre of the block outwards, sew the strips in sequence, starting with the 1½ in. (3.8 cm) B strip and the A square. Next, sew the 2 in. (5 cm) B strip across the top of that unit and the 2 in. (5 cm) A strip across the base. Take care to keep the ¼ in. (6 mm) seam allowances accurate when sewing so many narrow strips.

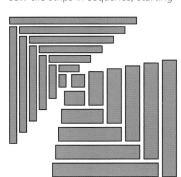

15 Kasuri nijū kaku
(Kasuri double square)

Inspired by traditional Japanese kasuri (ikat) woven fabrics.

A

B

C

CUTTING LIST

A   Two 5½ x 1 in. (14 x 2.5 cm) strips.

A   Two 6½ x 1 in. (16.5 x 2.5 cm) strips.

A   One 3½ in. (8.9 cm) square.

B   Four 6½ x 2 in. (16.5 x 5 cm) strips.

B   Four 3½ x 1½ in. (8.9 x 3.8 cm) strips.

C   Four 2 in. (5 cm) squares.

C   Four 1½ in. (3.8 cm) squares.

Construction

Sew the block, using the diagram as a guide. Start from the centre and work outwards. Take care to keep the ¼ in. (6 mm) seam allowances accurate when sewing the narrow strips.

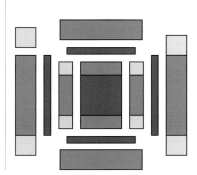

16 Kasuri kawari igeta
(Kasuri well curb variation)

Inspired by traditional Japanese kasuri (ikat) woven fabrics.

CUTTING LIST

A
B
C
D

A Four 3½ x 2½ in. (8.9 x 6.4 cm) strips.
A Two 3½ x 1 in. (8.9 x 2.5 cm) strips.
A Ten 2½ x 1 in. (6.4 x 2.5 cm) strips.
A Eight 1½ x 1 in. (3.8 x 2.5 cm) strips.
B Four 3½ x 1½ in. (8.9 x 3.8 cm) strips.
B Eight 2½ x 1½ in. (6.4 x 3.8 cm) strips.
C Eight 1½ in. (3.8 cm) squares.
D One 2½ in. (6.4 cm) square.

Construction

Sew the block, using the diagram as a guide. Make the corner and centre units first. Sew the pieces together into strips, then sew the strips together to complete the block.

17 Kasuri taikaku
(Kasuri diagonal)

Inspired by traditional Japanese kasuri (ikat) woven fabrics.

CUTTING LIST

A
B

A Four 7½ x 1½ in. (19 x 3.8 cm) strips.
A Four 5½ x 1½ in. (14 x 3.8 cm) strips.
A Four 3½ x 1½ in. (8.9 x 3.8 cm) strips.
A Four 1½ in. (3.8 cm) squares.
B One 3½ x 1½ in. (8.9 x 3.8 cm) strip.
B Fourteen 1½ in. (3.8 cm) squares.

Construction

Sew the block, using the diagram as a guide. Start from the centre and work outwards, making the centre cross unit first.

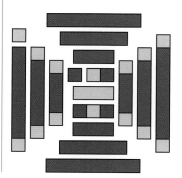

18 Kawari kasuri taikaku
(Kasuri diagonal variation)

Inspired by traditional Japanese kasuri (ikat) woven fabrics.

19 Kasuri gaikaku
(Kasuri enclosure)

Inspired by traditional Japanese kasuri (ikat) woven fabrics.

A
B
C

CUTTING LIST

A   Four 7½ x 1½ in. (19 x 3.8 cm) strips.
A   Four 5½ x 1½ in. (14 x 3.8 cm) strips.
A   Four 3½ x 1½ in. (8.9 x 3.8 cm) strips.
B   Two 2 in. (5 cm) squares.
B   Twelve 1½ in. (3.8 cm) squares.
C   Two 2 in. (5 cm) squares.

A
B

CUTTING LIST

A   Twelve 3½ x 1½ in. (8.9 x 3.8 cm) strips.
A   Sixteen 1½ in. (3.8 cm) squares.
B   One 3½ x 1½ in. (8.9 x 3.8 cm) strip.
B   Twenty-six 1½ in. (3.8 cm) squares.

Construction

Sew the block, using the diagram as a guide. Start from the centre and work outwards, making the centre four-patch unit using the B and C 2 in. (5 cm) squares first.

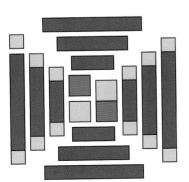

Construction

Sew the block, using the diagram as a guide. Start from the centre and work outwards, making the centre cross unit first.

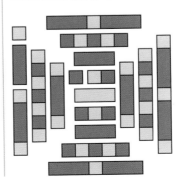

20 Kasuri jūji to kaku
(Kasuri cross and square)

Inspired by traditional Japanese kasuri (ikat) woven fabrics.

A
B
C

CUTTING LIST

A   Eight 3½ x 1½ in. (8.9 x 3.8 cm) strips.
A   Four 2½ x 1½ in. (6.4 x 3.8 cm) strips.
B   Eight 3½ x 1½ in. (8.9 x 3.8 cm) strips.
B   Eight 2½ x 1½ in. (6.4 x 3.8 cm) strips.
B   Five 1½ in. (3.8 cm) squares.
C   Four 1½ in. (3.8 cm) squares.

Construction

Sew the block, using the diagram as a guide. Sew the four square units separately, starting at the centre of each unit and sewing the strips in sequence. Sew the units together with the sashing strips, then add the border.

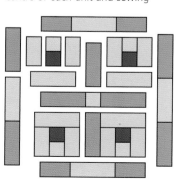

21 Kasuri jūji
(Kasuri crosses)

Inspired by traditional Japanese kasuri (ikat) woven fabrics.

A
B

CUTTING LIST

A   Four 5½ x 1½ in. (14 x 3.8 cm) strips.
A   Four 2½ x 1½ in. (6.4 x 3.8 cm) strips.
A   Sixteen 1½ in. (3.8 cm) squares.
B   Four 3½ x 1½ in. (8.9 x 3.8 cm) strips.
B   Four 2½ x 1½ in. (6.4 x 3.8 cm) strips.
B   Seventeen 1½ in. (3.8 cm) squares.

Construction

Sew the block, using the diagram as a guide. Sew the four square units separately. Start by sewing an A and B square together, then add a 2½ x 1½ in. (6.4 x 3.8 cm) B strip. Sew the finished units into the central cross design. Sew the remaining pieces together into strips, then complete the block from the centre outwards.

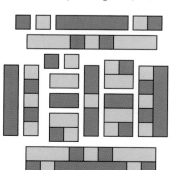

Project 1
Cushion

Using only four blocks, it is best to choose
closely coordinated fabrics for this cushion.
The selected blocks – clockwise from top left:
21, 18, 20 and 17 – are all based on kasuri (ikat)
woven fabric designs. The cushion measures
18 in. (45.7 cm) square.

YOU WILL NEED

- Four blocks of your choice.
- One 20 in. (50.8 cm) square of wadding.
- One 20 in. (50.8 cm) square of calico to
  back the patchwork panel.
- Two 18½ x 11 in. (47 x 27.9 cm) pieces
  of fabric for cushion back.
- One 18 in. (45.7 cm) cushion pad.

Construction

1 Sew the blocks together.
Layer and tack the cushion top,
wadding and calico (page 29).
Quilt the patchwork panel; this
cushion was machine quilted
in the ditch (page 30). Trim the
wadding and calico to match the
patchwork panel. Overlock all
around, or use a straight stitch
followed by a zigzag.

2 Sew a narrow hem on one long
side of each cushion back piece.
Overlock or zigzag the three raw
edges. Place the patchwork panel
and one of the backing pieces
right sides together and pin.

3 Place the second backing piece
right sides together, overlapping
the first piece, and pin. Machine
sew around the edge, using a
¼ in. (6 mm) seam allowance.
Clip the corners diagonally to
about ⅛ in. (3 mm) from the
edge and turn right side out.
Make sure that the corners are
well turned out. Insert the
cushion pad through the gap.

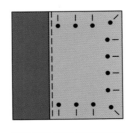

STEP 2

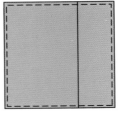

STEP 3

ENVELOPE-BACKED CUSHIONS

An overlap of 2–3 in. (5–7.6 cm) is
sufficient to allow you to insert a cushion
pad, but without the overlap gaping
open afterwards. If it does gape, sew
buttonholes on the outer panel and
buttons on the inner panel.

22 Yottsu igeta
(Four well curbs)

Inspired by geometric
kamon (family crests).

A
B
C

CUTTING LIST

A   Four 4¼ x 1¼ in. (10.8 x 3.2 cm) strips.
A   Four 1¾ x 1¼ in. (4.4 x 3.2 cm) strips.
A   Eight 1 x 1¼ in. (2.5 x 3.2 cm) strips.
B   Cut all of the above again in this fabric.
C   Two 9½ x 1 in. (24 x 2.5 cm) strips.
C   Three 8½ x 1 in. (21.6 x 2.5 cm) strips.
C   Two 4¼ x 1 in. (10.8 x 2.5 cm) strips.
C   Sixteen 1¾ x 1 in. (4.4 x 2.5 cm) strips.
C   Four 1¾ in. (4.4 cm) squares.
C   Sixteen 1 in. (2.5 cm) squares.

Construction

Sew the block, using the diagram as a guide. Sew the four square units separately. Sew the pieces together into strips, then sew the strips together to complete each unit. Sew the units together with the sashing strips, then add the border. Take care to keep the ¼ in. (6 mm) seam allowances accurate when sewing so many narrow strips.

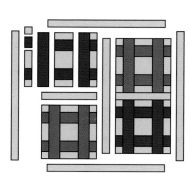

23 Ni mochiai kadotate igeta
(Interlocked corner well curbs)

Inspired by geometric
kamon (family crests).

A
B

CUTTING LIST

A   One 9½ x 1½ in. (24 x 3.8 cm) strip.
A   Four 4½ x 1½ in. (11.4 x 3.8 cm) strips.
A   Two 3 x 1½ in. (7.6 x 3.8 cm) strips.
A   Six 1 x 1½ in. (2.5 x 3.8 cm) strips.
B   Six 3 x 1 in. (7.6 x 2.5 cm) strips.
B   Two 2½ x 1 in. (6.4 x 2.5 cm) strips.
B   Two 4 in. (10.2 cm) squares.
B   Two 3 in. (7.6 cm) squares.
B   Six 1 in. (2.5 cm) squares.

Construction

Sew the block, using the diagram as a guide. Sew each corner unit of the block separately, then sew the units together with the sashing strips.

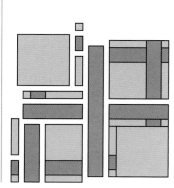

24 Hira izutsu ni kugi
(Flat well curb nail)

Inspired by geometric kamon (family crests).

CUTTING LIST

A Four 5½ x 1½ in. (14 x 3.8 cm) strips.
A Two 3⅜ in. (8.6 cm) squares, halved diagonally.
A Two 2 in. (5 cm) squares, halved diagonally.
A Four 1½ in. (3.8 cm) squares.
B Two 9½ x 1½ in. (24 x 3.8 cm) strips.
B Two 5½ x 1½ in. (14 x 3.8 cm) strips.
B Four 1½ in. (3.8 cm) squares.
B Four trapezoids using template 24 (page 111).

Construction

Using the triangles and trapezoids, sew each quarter of the centre unit separately to make four squares. Sew the squares together to complete the centre unit. Assemble and sew the borders to compete the block.

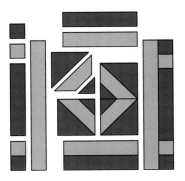

25 Chigai igeta
(Staggered igeta)

Inspired by geometric kamon (family crests).

CUTTING LIST

A One 1½ in. (3.8 cm) strip in these lengths:
   7½, 5½ and 3½ in. (19, 14 and 8.9 cm).
A Seven 1½ in. (3.8 cm) squares.
B One 7½ x 1½ in. (19 x 3.8 cm) strip.
B Two 5½ x 1½ in. (14 x 3.8 cm) strips.
B One 3½ x 1½ in. (8.9 x 3.8 cm) strip.
B Four 1½ in. (3.8 cm) squares.
C Four 3½ x 1½ in. (8.9 x 3.8 cm) strips.
C Two 2½ in. (6.4 cm) squares.
C Fifteen 1½ in. (3.8 cm) squares.

Construction

Sew the block, using the diagram as a guide. Sew the pieces together into strips, then sew the strips together to complete the block.

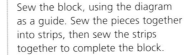

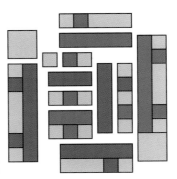

26 Ichimatsu yotsu me
(Four checked squares)

Inspired by geometric kamon (family crests).

A

B

CUTTING LIST
A   Eight 1⅝ x 3½ in. (4.1 x 8.9 cm) strips.
A   Eight 1⅝ x 1¼ in. (4.1 x 3.2 cm) strips.
B   Five 3½ in. (8.9 cm) squares.
B   Four 1¼ in. (3.2 cm) squares.

Construction
Sew the block, using the diagram as a guide. Sew the four pieced square units separately. Sew the units together into strips, then sew the strips together to complete the block.

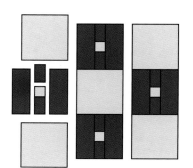

ALTERNATIVE DESIGN
Use assorted fabrics for each pieced square unit for a scrap look.

27 Hira yotsu me
(Four flat squares)

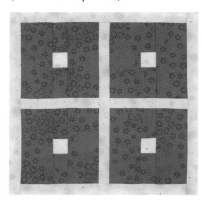

Inspired by geometric kamon (family crests).

A

B

CUTTING LIST
A   Eight 4¼ x 2 in. (10.8 x 5 cm) strips.
A   Eight 1¼ x 2 in. (3.2 x 5 cm) strips.
B   Two 9½ x 1 in. (24 x 2.5 cm) strips.
B   Three 8½ x 1 in. (21.6 x 2.5 cm) strips.
B   Two 4¼ x 1 in. (10.8 x 2.5 cm) strips.
B   Four 1¼ in. (3.2 cm) squares.

Construction
Sew the block, using the diagram as a guide. Sew the four square units separately. Sew the units together with the sashing strips, then add the border. Take care to keep the ¼ in. (6 mm) seam allowances accurate when sewing so many narrow strips.

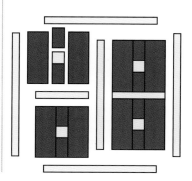

ALTERNATIVE DESIGN
Use assorted fabrics for each square unit for a scrap look.

28 Kokonotsu me
(Nine squares)

Inspired by geometric kamon (family crests).

 A

 B

 C

CUTTING LIST

A   Eighteen 1½ x 3 in. (3.8 x 7.6 cm) strips.
A   Eighteen 1½ x 1 in. (3.8 x 2.5 cm) strips.
B   Two 9½ x ⅞ in. (24 x 2.2 cm) strips.
B   Four 8¾ x ⅞ in. (22.2 x 2.2 cm) strips.
B   Six 3 x ⅞ in. (7.6 x 2.2 cm) strips.
C   Nine 1 in. (2.5 cm) squares.

Construction

Sew the block, using the diagram as a guide. Sew the nine square units separately. Sew the units together with the sashing strips, then add the border. Take care to keep the ¼ in. (6 mm) seam allowances accurate when sewing so many narrow strips.

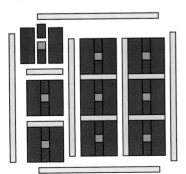

ALTERNATIVE DESIGN
Use assorted fabrics for each square unit for a scrap look.

29 Tsunagi kokonotsu me
(Linked nine squares)

Inspired by geometric kamon (family crests).

A

B

C

CUTTING LIST

A   Eighteen 2⅝ x 1¼ in. (6.7 x 3.2 cm) strips.
A   Eighteen 1⅛ x 1¼ in. (2.9 x 3.2 cm) strips.
B   One 4¼ in. (10.8 cm) squares, quartered diagonally.
B   Four 2⅝ in. (6.7 cm) squares.
B   Four 2⅜ in. (6 cm) squares, halved diagonally.
C   Nine 1⅛ in. (2.9 cm) squares.

Construction

Sew the block, using the diagram as a guide. Sew the nine pieced square units separately. Sew the units together into strips, then sew the strips together to complete the block. Take care not to stretch the bias edges of the triangles as you sew. Sew the corner triangles last.

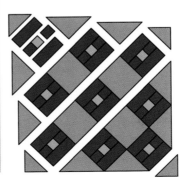

30 Kasane itsutsu me
(Five layered squares)

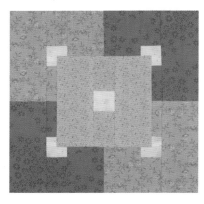

Inspired by geometric kamon (family crests).

 A

 B

 C

 D

CUTTING LIST

- A   Two 5 x 2¼ in. (12.7 x 5.7 cm) strips.
- A   Two 2¾ x 2¼ in. (7 x 5.7 cm) strips.
- A   Two 2¼ x 1½ in. (5.7 x 3.8 cm) strips.
- A   Two 2¼ x 1 in. (5.7 x 2.5 cm) strips.
- B   Cut all of the above again in this fabric.
- C   Two 5 x 2¼ in. (12.7 x 5.7 cm) strips.
- C   Two 2¼ x 1½ in. (5.7 x 3.8 cm) strips.
- D   Four 1½ x 1 in. (3.8 x 2.5 cm) strips.
- D   One 1½ in. (3.8 cm) square.
- D   Four 1 in. (2.5 cm) squares.

Construction

Sew the block, using the diagram as a guide. Sew the pieces together into strips, then sew the strips together to complete the block, starting from the centre and working outwards.

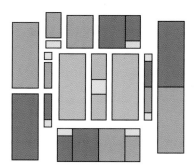

31 Kasegi yotsu me
(Four square working)

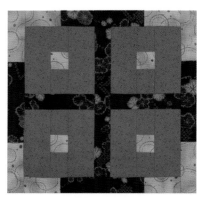

Inspired by geometric kamon (family crests).

A

B

C

CUTTING LIST

- A   One 8 x 1¼ in. (20.3 x 3.2 cm) strip.
- A   Four 4½ x 1¼ in. (11.4 x 3.2 cm) strips.
- A   Two 3⅞ x 1¼ in. (9.8 x 3.2 cm) strips.
- B   Eight 3⅞ x 1¾ in. (9.8 x 4.4 cm) strips.
- B   Eight 1¾ x 1⅜ in. (4.4 x 3.5 cm) strips.
- C   Four 3 x 1¼ in. (7.6 x 3.2 cm) strips.
- C   Four 2¼ x 1¼ in. (5.7 x 3.2 cm) strips.
- C   Four 1⅜ in. (3.5 cm) squares.

Construction

Sew the block, using the diagram as a guide. Sew the four square units separately, then sew the units together with the sashing strips. Assemble and sew the border to compete the block.

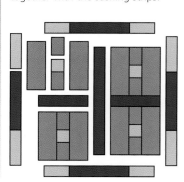

32 Kasuri kasane koshi
(Kasuri layered check)

Inspired by traditional Japanese kasuri (ikat) woven fabrics.

CUTTING LIST

A

B

C

A   Two 5 x 2¾ in. (12.7 x 7 cm) strips.
A   Two 2¾ in. (7 cm) squares.
A   Sixteen 1 in. (2.5 cm) squares.
B   Two 5 x 2¾ in. (12.7 x 7 cm) strips.
B   Two 2¾ in. (7 cm) squares.
C   Five 5 x 1 in. (12.7 x 2.5 cm) strips.
C   Twenty 1 in. (2.5 cm) squares.

Construction

Sew the block, using the diagram as a guide. Sew the centre grid unit first. Sew the pieces together into strips, then sew the strips together to complete the unit. Assemble and sew the border to complete the block.

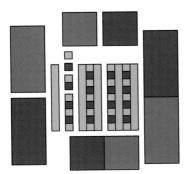

PATCHWORK NOTES
For a simpler block, replace the centre grid unit with a 5 in. (12.7 cm) square of checked fabric.

Mix & match
quilt designs

Chequerboards with two blocks

▲ Blocks 19 and 32 make a double chequerboard effect with strong diagonals.

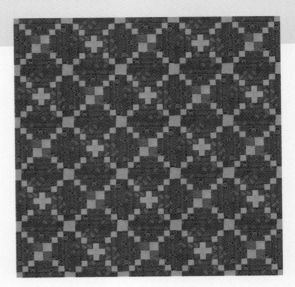

▲ Blocks 17 and 18 are alternated in a simple diagonal crossed chain.

33 Tokiwa gaki
(Ordinary fence)

Inspired by geometric kamon (family crests).

34 Kunojiki sujikai
(Simplified right-angle braces)

Inspired by geometric kamon (family crests).

CUTTING LIST

A
B

A Five 4½ x 1½ in. (11.4 x 3.8 cm) strips.
A Two 4½ x 1 in. (11.4 x 2.5 cm) strips.
A Fourteen 1½ x 1 in. (3.8 x 2.5 cm) strips.
A Ten 1½ in. (3.8 cm) squares.
A Four 1 in. (2.5 cm) squares.
B Six 9½ x 1 in. (24 x 2.5 cm) strips.
B Twenty 1½ x 1 in. (3.8 x 2.5 cm) strips.
B Eight 1 in. (2.5 cm) squares.

CUTTING LIST

A
B
C

A One 1 in. (2.5 cm) strip in these lengths: 9½, 8½, 6 and 3½ in. (24, 21.6, 15.2 and 8.9 cm); plus six 2½ in. (6.4 cm).
A Five 1 in. (2.5 cm) squares.
B One 1 in. (2.5 cm) strip in these lengths: 8¼, 6½, 4¾ and 3 in. (21, 16.5, 12 and 7.6 cm); plus six 1¾ in. (4.4 cm) and four 1¼ in. (3.2 cm).
C Twelve 2½ x 1¾ in. (6.4 x 4.4 cm) strips.
C Six 2½ x 1¼ in. (6.4 x 3.2 cm) strips.
C 1 in. (2.5 cm) strips in these lengths: eight 1¾ in. (4.4 cm) and four 1¼ in. (3.2 cm).

Construction

Sew the block, using the diagram as a guide. Sew the pieces together into strips, then sew the strips together to complete the block.

Take care to keep the ¼ in. (6 mm) seam allowances accurate when sewing so many narrow strips.

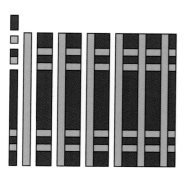

ALTERNATIVE DESIGN
Use this block as a backdrop for appliquéed flowers and leaves.

Construction

Sew the block, using the diagram as a guide. Sew the pieces together into units, then sew the units together to complete the block,

starting at the top right-hand corner. Take care to keep the ¼ in. (6 mm) seam allowances accurate when sewing so many narrow strips.

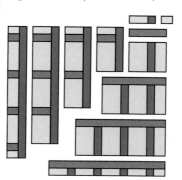

35 Kakuyose
(Parquetry angles)

Inspired by geometric kamon (family crests).

36 Kasuri igeta no.1
(Kasuri well curb no.1)

Inspired by traditional Japanese kasuri (ikat) woven fabrics.

CUTTING LIST

A   Two 1 in. (2.5 cm) strips in these lengths: 6½, 6, 5½, 5, 4½ and 4 in. (16.5, 15.2, 14, 12.7, 11.4 and 10.2 cm).
A   One 3½ in. (8.9 cm) square.
A   Eighteen 1 in. (2.5 cm) squares.
B   One 1 in. (2.5 cm) strip in these lengths: 9, 8½, 8, 7½, 7, 6½, 6, 5½, 5, 4½, 4 and 3½ in. (22.9, 21.6, 20.3, 19, 17.8, 16.5, 15.2, 14, 12.7, 11.4, 10.2 and 8.9 cm).
B   Eighteen 1 in. (2.5 cm) squares.

CUTTING LIST

A   Two 8½ x 2 in. (21.6 x 5 cm) strips.
A   Two 2½ x 2 in. (6.4 x 5 cm) strips.
A   Four 2 x 1½ in. (5 x 3.8 cm) strips.
A   Eight 2 in. (5 cm) squares.
A   One 1½ in. (3.8 cm) square.
B   Eight 2 x 1 in. (5 x 2.5 cm) strips.
B   Twenty-four 1½ x 1 in. (3.8 x 2.5 cm) strips.
C   Thirty-two 1 in. (2.5 cm) squares.

Construction

Sew the block, using the diagram as a guide. Using one A strip of each length, sew three 1 in. (2.5 cm) squares of each fabric to the ends of each strip. Working from the centre of the block outwards, sew the strips to the top and left of the large A square in sequence, starting with the 3½ in. (8.9 cm) B strip across the top of the square. Repeat with the bottom and right strips. Take care to keep the ¼ in. (6 mm) seam allowances accurate when sewing so many narrow strips.

Construction

Sew the block, using the diagram as a guide. Build up the smaller pieces into units first. Sew the units together into strips, then sew the strips together to complete the block. Take care to keep the ¼ in. (6 mm) seam allowances accurate when sewing so many small pieces.

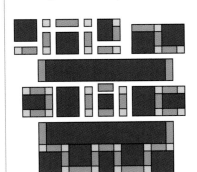

37 Kasuri igeta no.2
(Kasuri well curb no.2)

Inspired by traditional Japanese kasuri (ikat) woven fabrics.

A		
B		
C		
D		

CUTTING LIST

A Four 1½ x 2 in. (3.8 x 5 cm) strips.
A Eight 2 in. (5 cm) squares.
A One 1½ in. (3.8 cm) square.
B Twelve 1½ x 1 in. (3.8 x 2.5 cm) strips.
C Twenty-four 2 x 1 in. (5 x 2.5 cm) strips.
C Twenty-four 1½ x 1 in. (3.8 x 2.5 cm) strips.
D Thirty-two 1 in. (2.5 cm) squares.

Construction

Sew the block, using the diagram as a guide. Build up the smaller pieces into units first. Sew the units together into strips, then sew the strips together to complete the block. Take care to keep the ¼ in. (6 mm) seam allowances accurate when sewing so many small pieces.

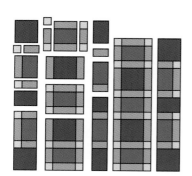

38 Kasuri jūji hishi
(Kasuri diamond crosses)

Inspired by traditional Japanese kasuri (ikat) woven fabrics.

A		
B		

CUTTING LIST

A Four 2½ x 2 in. (6.4 x 5 cm) strips.
A Two 9½ x 1¾ in. (24 x 4.4 cm) strips.
A Two 7 x 1¾ in. (17.8 x 4.4 cm) strips.
A Four 3 x 1 in. (7.6 x 2.5 cm) strips.
A Four 1½ x 1 in. (3.8 x 2.5 cm) strips.
A Four 1½ in. (3.8 cm) squares.
A Twenty-eight 1 in. (2.5 cm) squares.
B Four 2 x 1 in. (5 x 2.5 cm) strips.
B One 2 in. (5 cm) square.
B Twenty-eight 1 in. (2.5 cm) squares.

Construction

Sew the block, using the diagram as a guide. Build up the smaller pieces into units first. Sew the units together into strips, then sew the strips together, starting from the centre and working outwards. Add the border to complete the block. Take care to keep the ¼ in. (6 mm) seam allowances accurate when sewing so many small pieces.

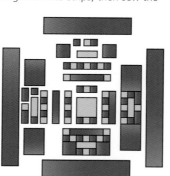

39 Kasuri hoshi
(Kasuri star)

Inspired by traditional Japanese kasuri (ikat) woven fabrics.

A

B

CUTTING LIST

A Two 9½ x 1¾ in. (24 x 4.4 cm) strips.
A Two 7 x 1¾ in. (17.8 x 4.4 cm) strips.
A Eight 2 x 1 in. (5 x 2.5 cm) strips.
A Four 1½ x 1 in. (3.8 x 2.5 cm) strips.
A Four 1½ in. (3.8 cm) squares.
A Twenty-eight 1 in. (2.5 cm) squares.
B One 2 in. (5 cm) square.
B Twelve 1½ in. (3.8 cm) squares.
B Thirty-six 1 in. (2.5 cm) squares.

Construction

Sew the block, using the diagram as a guide. Build up the smaller pieces into units first. Sew the units together into strips, then sew the strips together, starting from the centre and working outwards. Add the border to complete the block. Take care to keep the ¼ in. (6 mm) seam allowances accurate when sewing so many small pieces.

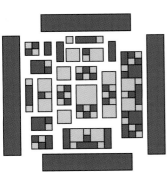

40 Kasuri hana musubi
(Kasuri flower knot)

Inspired by traditional Japanese kasuri (ikat) woven fabrics.

A

B

CUTTING LIST

A Two 9½ x 1¼ in. (24 x 3.2 cm) strips.
A Two 8 x 1¼ in. (20.3 x 3.2 cm) strips.
A Twenty-eight 1½ x 1 in. (3.8 x 2.5 cm) strips.
A Forty 1 in. (2.5 cm) squares.
B One 3 x 2 in. (7.6 x 5 cm) strip.
B Eight 2½ x 1 in. (6.4 x 2.5 cm) strips.
B Six 2 x 1 in. (5 x 2.5 cm) strips.
B Eight 1½ x 1 in. (3.8 x 2.5 cm) strips.
B Forty-eight 1 in. (2.5 cm) squares.

Construction

Sew the block, using the diagram as a guide. Build up the smaller pieces into units first. Sew the units together into strips, then sew the strips together. Add the border to complete the block. Take care to keep the ¼ in. (6 mm) seam allowances accurate when sewing so many small pieces.

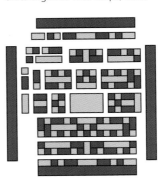

41 Kasuri fuzoku no igeta

(Kasuri enclosed igeta)

Inspired by traditional Japanese kasuri (ikat) woven fabrics.

A

B

CUTTING LIST

A Two 8 x 1¼ in. (20.3 x 3.2 cm) strips.
A Two 9½ x 1¼ in. (24 x 3.2 cm) strips.
A Eight 2 x 1½ in. (5 x 3.8 cm) strips.
A Sixty-five 1 in. (2.5 cm) squares.
B Two 3 x 1 in. (7.6 x 2.5 cm) strips.
B Twenty 2 x 1 in. (5 x 2.5 cm) strips.
B Forty-two 1 in. (2.5 cm) squares.

Construction

Sew the block, using the diagram as a guide. Build up the smaller pieces into units first. Sew the units together into strips, then sew the strips together. Add the border to complete the block. Take care to keep the ¼ in. (6 mm) seam allowances accurate when sewing so many small pieces.

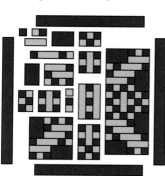

42 Kasuri fuzoku no kaku

(Kasuri enclosed square)

Inspired by traditional Japanese kasuri (ikat) woven fabrics.

A

B

CUTTING LIST

A Two 9½ x ¾ in. (24 x 1.9 cm) strips.
A Two 9 x ¾ in. (22.9 x 1.9 cm) strips.
A Eight 1 in. (2.5 cm) strips in these lengths: 2½, 2, and 1½ in. (6.4, 5, and 3.8 cm).
A Four 2 in. (5 cm) and four 1½ in. (3.8 cm) squares.
A Forty-five 1 in. (2.5 cm) squares.
B Twelve 2 x 1 in. (5 x 2.5 cm) strips.
B Six 1½ x 1 in. (3.8 x 2.5 cm) strips.
B Four 1½ in. (3.8 cm) squares.
B Fifty-six 1 in. (2.5 cm) squares.

Construction

Sew the block, using the diagram as a guide. Build up the smaller pieces into units first. Sew the units together into strips, then sew the strips together. Add the border to complete the block. Take care to keep the ¼ in. (6 mm) seam allowances accurate when sewing so many small pieces.

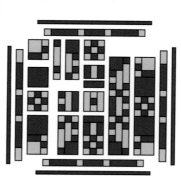

43 Kasuri fuzoku no hana
(Kasuri enclosed flower)

Inspired by traditional Japanese kasuri (ikat) woven fabrics.

44 Nagai kikkō
(Long hexagons)

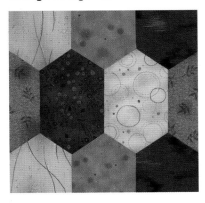

Inspired by traditional Japanese patterns and woven kimono fabrics.

CUTTING LIST

A   Two 9½ x ¾ in. (24 x 1.9 cm) strips.
A   Two 9 x ¾ in. (22.9 x 1.9 cm) strips.
A   Four 2½ x 1½ in. (6.4 x 3.8 cm) strips.
A   Four 1½ x 1 in. (3.8 x 2.5 cm) strips.
A   Eight 1½ in. (3.8 cm) squares.
A   Seventy-three 1 in. (2.5 cm) squares.
B   Four 3 x 1 in. (7.6 x 2.5 cm) strips.
B   Ten 2 x 1 in. (5 x 2.5 cm) strips.
B   Thirty-four 1½ x 1 in. (3.8 x 2.5 cm) strips.
B   Twenty-six 1 in. (2.5 cm) squares.

CUTTING LIST

A   One piece from template 44a (page 108).
B   One piece from template 44a (page 108).
C   Two pieces from template 44b (page 109).
D   Two pieces from template 44c (page 109).
E   Two pieces from template 44c (page 109).
F   Two pieces from template 44c (page 109).

Construction

Sew the block, using the diagram as a guide. Build up the smaller pieces into units first. Sew the units together into strips, then sew the strips together. Add the border to complete the block. Take care to keep the ¼ in. (6 mm) seam allowances accurate when sewing so many small pieces.

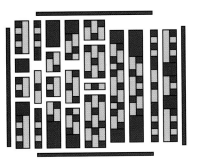

Construction

Sew the block, using the diagram as a guide. Sew the pieces into rows, then sew the rows together, using inset seams (see page 22). Take care not to stretch the bias edges when sewing hexagons.

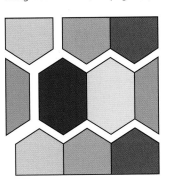

45 Komochi kume igeta
(Grouped well-curb whirlpool)

Inspired by geometric kamon (family crests).

CUTTING LIST

A   Four 6 x 3 in. (15.2 x 7.6 cm) strips.
A   Four 1½ x 3 in. (3.8 x 7.6 cm) strips.
B   Four 2½ x 1½ in. (6.4 x 3.8 cm) strips.
B   One 2½ in. (6.4 cm) square.
B   Four 1½ in. (3.8 cm) squares.

Construction

Sew the block, using the diagram as a guide. Sew the four outer units separately. Begin sewing one unit to the centre square, using the part-sewn seam method, as shown in red (page 22). Continue adding the units with this method to complete the block. Press all part-sewn seams towards the outer edges of the block.

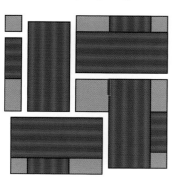

46 Chigai kaku
(Different angles)

Inspired by geometric kamon (family crests).

CUTTING LIST

A   Two 7 x 1½ in. (17.8 x 3.8 cm) strips.
A   One 5 x 1½ in. (12.7 x 3.8 cm) strip.
A   One 2½ x 1½ in. (6.4 x 3.8 cm) strip.
A   One 2 x 1½ in. (5 x 3.8 cm) strip.
B   Cut all of the above again in this fabric.
C   Two 5 x 2 in. (12.7 x 5 cm) strips.
C   Two 3½ x 2 in. (8.9 x 5 cm) strips.
C   Two 3 in. (7.6 cm) squares.
C   One 2½ in. (6.4 cm) square.

Construction

Sew the block, using the diagram as a guide. Make the centre unit first, sewing one A and one B 2½ x 1½ in. (6.4 x 3.8 cm) strip to opposite sides of the smaller C square. Sew one A and one B 7 x 1½ in. (17.8 x 3.8 cm) strip to opposite sides of this unit, using the part-sewn seam method, as shown in red (page 22). Continue adding pieces with this method to complete the block.

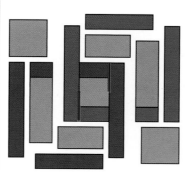

Project 2
Lap quilt

Make nine patchwork blocks – 4, 22, 23, 25, 26, 28, 31, 45 and 46 – go further by alternating them with plain blocks and setting the blocks on point. The cool colourway calms the design. The finished quilt is 48 in. (121.9 cm) square.

YOU WILL NEED

- Nine blocks of your choice.
- Four 9⅞ in. (25 cm) squares of woven plaid.
- Four 9⅞ in. (25 cm) squares of woven plaid, halved diagonally.
- One 10¼ in. (26 cm) square of woven plaid, quartered diagonally.
- Four 43 x 5 in. (109.2 x 12.7 cm) border strips.
- One 50 in. (127 cm) square of backing fabric.
- One 50 in. (127 cm) square of wadding.
- Two 48 x 1½ in. (121.9 x 3.8 cm) strips for binding.
- Two 50 x 1½ in. (127 x 3.8 cm) strips for binding.

Construction

1 Arrange the blocks and plaid pieces, then machine sew the quilt top together. Press the seams towards the plaid pieces. Sew the border strips around the quilt, using the part-sewn seam method (page 22).

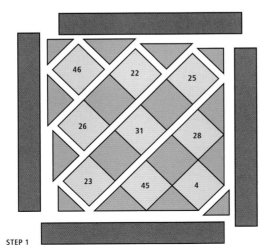

STEP 1

2 Layer and tack the patchwork, wadding and backing (page 29). Quilt the panel. This lap quilt was hand quilted in the ditch around the patchwork blocks (page 30); the plain blocks were big-stitch quilted (page 31), using block 108 as a design. Trim the wadding and backing to match the patchwork panel and machine sew.

3 Bind the quilt using the binding strips.

47 Kadotate karami inazuma
(Entwined angle lightning spiral)

Inspired by geometric kamon (family crests).

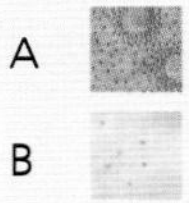

CUTTING LIST

A Two 8½ x 1½ in. (21.6 x 3.8 cm) strips.
A Two 8¼ x 1½ in. (21 x 3.8 cm) strips.
A Two 1⅜ in. (3.5 cm) strips in these lengths: 6⅜, 5⅞, 4⅛, 3⅝ and 2¾ in. (16.2, 14.9, 10.5, 9.2 and 7 cm).
B Two ¾ in. (1.9 cm) strips in these lengths: 8½, 6⅜, 5⅞, 4⅛, 3⅝ and 1⅜ in. (21.6, 16.2, 14.9, 10.5, 9.2 and 3.5 cm).
B One 3 x ¾ in. (7.6 x 1.9 cm) strip.

Construction

Sew the block, using the diagram as a guide. Make the centre unit first, with the shortest A and B strips, joined at the centre with the 3 x ¾ in. (7.6 x 1.9 cm) B strip. Sew the A and B strips together in pairs. Sew the two 3⅝ in. (9.2 cm) long units to the top and bottom of the centre unit, using the part-sewn seam method, as shown in red (page 22). Continue adding strips with this method to complete the block. Press all seams towards the outer edges to reduce bulk. Take care to keep the ¼ in. (6 mm) seam allowances accurate when sewing so many narrow strips.

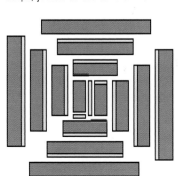

48 Kadotate ichimatsu inazuma
(Angled lightning spiral check)

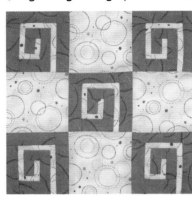

Inspired by geometric kamon (family crests).

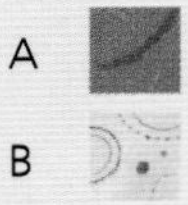

CUTTING LIST

A Five 3½ x 1⅛ in. (8.9 x 2.9 cm) strips.
A Ten 2⅞ x 1⅛ in. (7.3 x 2.9 cm) strips.
A Five 2 x 1⅛ in. (5 x 2.9 cm) strips.
A Five 2 x 1 in. (5 x 2.5 cm) strips.
A Ten 1¼ x 1 in. (3.2 x 2.5 cm) strips.
B Five 2⅞ x ¾ in. (7.3 x 1.9 cm) strips.
B Ten 2 x ¾ in. (5 x 1.9 cm) strips.
B Ten 1¼ x ¾ in. (3.2 x 1.9 cm) strips.
B Four 3½ in. (8.9 cm) squares.

Construction

Sew the block, using the diagram as a guide. Sew the five spiral units separately, starting at the centre with one 1¼ x 1 in. (3.2 x 2.5 cm) A strip and one 1¼ x ¾ in. (3.2 x 1.9 cm) B strip. Using the same size strips, sew another A strip across the top and another B strip across the bottom. Add the remaining strips in sequence. Press the seams towards the outer edges of the units. Sew the units together into strips of three, then sew the strips together to complete the block. Take care to keep the ¼ in. (6 mm) seam allowances accurate when sewing so many narrow strips.

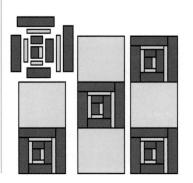

49 Futatsu kagi
(Two keys)

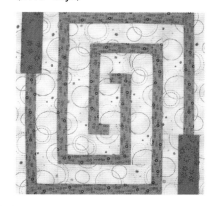

Inspired by geometric kamon (family crests).

 A
 B
 C

CUTTING LIST

A Two 3½ x 1½ in. (8.9 x 3.8 cm) strips.

B Two 1 in. (2.5 cm) strips in these lengths: 7½, 4½ and 3½ in. (19, 11.4 and 8.9 cm); plus four 6½ in. (16.5 cm).

B Two 1 in. (2.5 cm) squares.

C Two 1½ in. (3.8 cm) strips in these lengths: 5 and 2 in. (12.7 and 5 cm); plus four 6 in. (15.2 cm) and one 2½ in. (6.4 cm).

C Two 3½ x 1¼ in. (8.9 x 3.2 cm) strips.

C Two 6½ x 1 in. (16.5 x 2.5 cm) strips.

C Two 3½ x ¾ in. (8.9 x 1.9 cm) strips.

C Two 1 in. (2.5 cm) squares.

Construction

Sew the block, using the diagram as a guide. Start with the 2½ x 1½ in. (6.4 x 3.8 cm) C strip and the four 1 in. (2.5 cm)

B and C squares at the centre of the block. Sew the two 4½ x 1 in. (11.4 x 2.5 cm) B strips to either side, using the part-sewn seam method, as shown in red (page 22). Continue adding strips with this method to complete the block, adding the 'key handles' at the end. Take care to keep the ¼ in. (6 mm) seam allowances accurate when sewing so many small pieces.

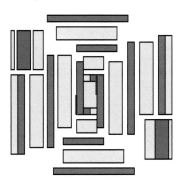

50 Izutsu kuzushi
(Simplified well curb)

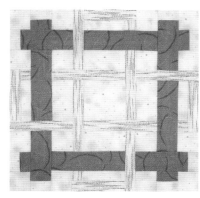

Inspired by geometric kamon (family crests).

 A
 B
C

CUTTING LIST

A Four 4 x 1½ in. (10.2 x 3.8 cm) strips.

A Four 3 x 1½ in. (7.6 x 3.8 cm) strips.

A Four 1½ x 1 in. (3.8 x 2.5 cm) strips.

B Four 1 in. (2.5 cm) strips in these lengths: 4, 3½ and 3 in. (10.2, 8.9 and 7.6 cm).

B Four 1 in. (2.5 cm) squares.

C Four 2½ x 1½ in. (6.4 x 3.8 cm) strips.

C Four 2½ x 1 in. (6.4 x 2.5 cm) strips.

C Eight 1½ x 1 in. (3.8 x 2.5 cm) strips.

C One 2½ in. (6.4 cm) and sixteen 1½ in. (3.8 cm) squares.

Construction

Sew the block, using the diagram as a guide. Begin by sewing the four 4 x 1 in. (10.2 x 2.5 cm) B strips to the large C square,

using the part-sewn seam method, as shown by the single red line (page 22). Sew the 3½ x 1 in. (8.9 x 2.5 cm) B strips, 2½ x 1½ in. (6.4 x 3.8 cm) C strips and four 1½ in. (3.8 cm) C squares into four separate units with part-sewn seams, as shown by the double red lines, and add to the centre unit. Make the side and corner units. Complete the block with more part-sewn seams.

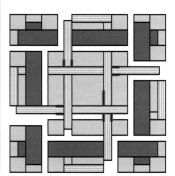

51 Kawari kumi sujikaki
(Paired braces variation)

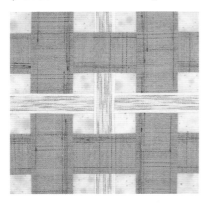

Inspired by geometric
kamon (family crests).

CUTTING LIST

 A

 B

 C

A   Four 4½ x 2½ in. (11.4 x 6.4 cm) strips.
A   Two 3½ x 2½ in. (8.9 x 6.4 cm) strips.
A   Four 1½ x 2½ in. (3.8 x 6.4 cm) strips.
B   Two 4½ x 1½ in. (11.4 x 3.8 cm) strips.
B   One 3½ x 1½ in. (8.9 x 3.8 cm) strip.
B   Two 1½ in. (3.8 cm) squares.
C   Sixteen 1½ in. (3.8 cm) squares.

Construction

Sew the block, using the diagram as a guide. Make the central unit first with four C squares and the B strips, using the part-sewn seam method, as shown in red (page 22). Make the top and bottom units and sew to the centre unit. Make and add the four corner units. Finish the part-sewn seams to complete the block.

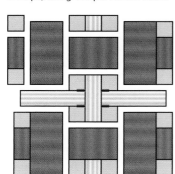

52 Kine izutsu
(Rice pestle well curb)

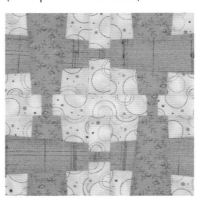

Inspired by geometric
kamon (family crests).

CUTTING LIST

 A

 B

 C

A   Two pieces from template 52a (page 110).
A   Two pieces from template 52b (page 110).
A   Two pieces from template 52c (page 110).
A   Two 1½ x 1 in. (3.8 x 2.5 cm) strips.
B   Cut all of the above again in this fabric.
C   Four pieces from each of these templates: 52d, 52e, 52f and 52g (all page 110).
C   One 5 x 1½ in. (12.7 x 3.8 cm) strip.
C   Six 2¼ x 1½ in. (5.7 x 3.8 cm) strips.

Construction

Sew the block, using the diagram as a guide. Sew each corner unit separately, taking care not to mix up the similar-sized background pieces d, e, f and g. Use the remaining pieces to make the sashing strips. Sew the units together with the sashing strips to complete the block.

53 Yamagata
(Mountain shape)

Inspired by traditional Japanese patterns and woven kimono fabrics. Also found as a background on Noh costume patterns.

  CUTTING LIST

A   Six 9½ x 2 in. (24 x 5 cm) strips.

Construction

Use a fabric with woven or printed wide stripes. Cut the strips at 45 degrees to the stripe pattern, lining up the stripes on adjacent strips to make a zigzag effect. Sew the block, using the diagram as a guide. Sew the strips together into pairs, then sew the pairs together to complete the block. Take care not to stretch the bias edges when sewing.

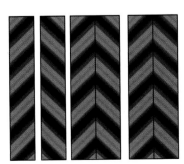

54 Yabane
(Arrow feather)

Inspired by traditional Japanese patterns and woven kimono fabrics.

A **CUTTING LIST**

B

A   Six 9½ x 1¾ in. (24 x 4.4 cm) strips.
B   Three 9½ x 1 in. (24 x 2.5 cm) strips.

Construction

Choose an A fabric with woven or printed wide stripes. Cut the strips at 45 degrees to the stripe pattern, offsetting the stripes on adjacent strips to make a feather effect. Sew the block, using the diagram as a guide. Take care not to stretch the bias edges when sewing.

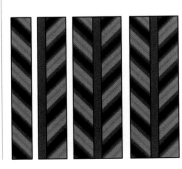

55 Awase yamagata
(Overlapped mountain shape)

Inspired by geometric kamon (family crests).

 A

 B

 C

CUTTING LIST

A   Four pieces from template 55a (page 109).
A   Four pieces from template 55b (page 109).
A   Four pieces from template 55c (page 109).
B   One 5¾ in. (14.6 cm) square, quartered diagonally.
B   One 4¼ in. (10.8 cm) square, quartered diagonally.
B   One 2¾ in. (7 cm) square, quartered diagonally.
C   One 5¾ in. (14.6 cm) square, quartered diagonally.
C   One 4¼ in. (10.8 cm) square, quartered diagonally.
C   One 2¾ in. (7 cm) square, quartered diagonally.

Construction

Match the stripe pattern when cutting out all the A pieces. Sew the block, using the diagram as a guide. Sew each quarter unit of the block separately, then sew the four units together. Take care not to stretch the bias edges on the triangles when sewing.

PATCHWORK NOTES
Two triangles cut from the largest and smallest squares will be left over, in both B and C fabrics, so this block is most economical when made in pairs.

56 Kumi sujikai
(Paired braces)

Inspired by geometric kamon (family crests).

 A

 B

CUTTING LIST

A   Two pieces from template 56a (page 112).
A   Two pieces from template 56b (page 112).
A   Four pieces from template 56c (page 113).
B   Two triangles from template 56d (page 112).
B   Two triangles from template 56e (page 112).
B   Two pieces from template 56f (page 113).
B   Two pieces from template 56f flipped (page 113).
B   One piece from template 56g (page 112).

Construction

Match the stripe pattern when cutting the A pieces. Sew the block, using the diagram as a guide. Sew the four triangular units separately.

Begin sewing the bottom unit to the centre lozenge, using the part-sewn seam method, as shown in red (page 22). Next sew the right unit, then the top unit, continuing with this method to complete the block. Take care not to stretch the bias edges when sewing.

PATCHWORK NOTES
If necessary, use a different fabric to cut the pieces from template 56c to achieve a woven effect.

57 Hanakaku
(Square flower)

Inspired by geometric kamon (family crests).

		CUTTING LIST
A	■	A Four pieces from template 57a (page 111).
B	■	B Four pieces from template 57b (page 111).
C	■	C Four pieces from template 57c (page 111).
		C Four pieces from template 57c flipped (page 111).

Construction

Sew the block, using the diagram as a guide. Sew the A and B pieces together in pairs, then sew pairs together to make the two halves of the flower. Add a pair of C pieces to the block corners on each half, using inset seams (page 22). Sew the two halves together and add the remaining C pieces. Take care not to stretch the bias edges when sewing.

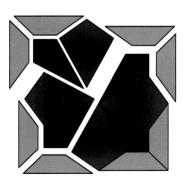

Mix & match
quilt designs

Linear arrangements

▲ From top to bottom, blocks 53, 67, 55, 66 and 54 are arranged in continuous rows.

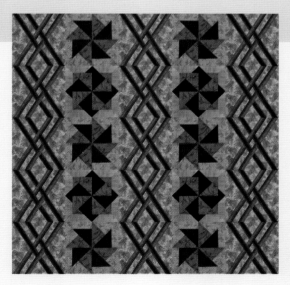

▲ Block 56 repeats to make three chains, with blocks 60 and 61 alternating in columns between the chains.

58 Tatami kamashiki
(Straw mat kettle trivet)

Inspired by geometric kamon (family crests).

CUTTING LIST

A
B

A   Six triangles from template 58a (page 114).
B   Two triangles from template 58b (page 114).
B   Two triangles from template 58b flipped (page 114).

Construction

Cut the A triangles so that the stripe pattern changes direction around the block. Note that these are isosceles triangles, not equilateral; the vertical edges are shorter. Sew the block, using the diagram as a guide. Sew the centre hexagon first, then add the corner triangles. Take care not to stretch the bias edges when sewing.

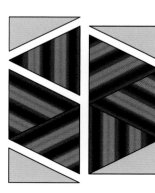

59 Rokkaku wakamatsu
(Young pine hexagon)

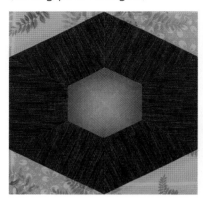

Inspired by geometric kamon (family crests).

CUTTING LIST

A
B
C

A   Two pieces from template 59a (page 115).
A   Two pieces from template 59b (page 115).
A   Two pieces from template 59b flipped (page 115).
B   One hexagon from template 59c (page 115).
C   Two triangles from template 58b (page 114).
C   Two triangles from template 58b flipped (page 114).

Construction

Cut the A pieces so that the stripe pattern radiates outwards around the block. Sew the block, using the diagram as a guide. Sew the two 59a pieces to the centre hexagon first. Add one 59b and one 59b flipped pieces to the top, using inset seams (page 22); do the same at the bottom. Sew the corner triangles last. Take care not to stretch the bias edges when sewing.

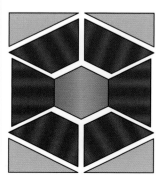

60 Yotsume guruma
(Quadruple wheel)

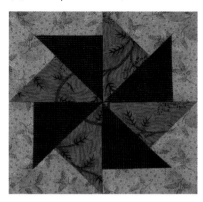

Inspired by geometric kamon (family crests).

CUTTING LIST

A

B

C

A   Two 4⅛ in. (10.5 cm) squares, halved diagonally.
B   One 5¾ in. (14.6 cm) square, quartered diagonally.
C   One 5¾ in. (14.6 cm) square, quartered diagonally.
C   Four pieces from template 60 (page 114).

Construction

Sew the block, using the diagram as a guide. Sew each quarter of the block separately, then sew the four quarter units together.

Take care not to stretch the bias edges when sewing.

PATCHWORK NOTES
Note that the A and B triangles are cut differently, so that the triangles continue the line of the fabric grain in the block.

61 Kasane yotsume guruma
(Layered quadruple wheel)

Inspired by geometric kamon (family crests).

CUTTING LIST

A

B

C

A   One 5¾ in. (14.6 cm) square, quartered diagonally.
A   Two 2⅛ in. (5.4 cm) squares, halved diagonally.
B   Two 4⅛ in. (10.5 cm) squares, halved diagonally.
B   One 3¼ in. (8.3 cm) square, quartered diagonally.
C   Eight pieces from template 61 (page 111).

Construction

Sew the block, using the diagram as a guide. Sew each quarter of the block separately, then sew the four quarter units together.

Take care not to stretch the bias edges when sewing.

PATCHWORK NOTES
Note that the A and B triangles are cut differently, so that the triangles continue the line of the fabric grain in the block.

62 Yottsu wakamatsu
(Four young pines)

Inspired by kamon (family crests) featuring plants, leaves and objects.

63 Shippō
(Seven treasures)

Inspired by ancient Japanese court designs.

A

B

C

CUTTING LIST

A   One 9½ in. (24 cm) square.

B   Four 4¼ in. (10.8 cm) squares.

C   One 8¼ x ¾ in. (21 x 1.9 cm) strip.

C   Two 4¼ x ¾ in. (10.8 x 1.9 cm) strips.

A

B

CUTTING LIST

A   One piece from template 63a (page 113).

A   Four pieces from template 63b (page 115).

B   Four pieces from template 63c (page 108).

Construction

Cut the B squares with the striped fabric on the bias. Sew the B squares and C strips together, using the diagram as a guide. Press the seams towards the squares. Cut an 8-in. (20.3-cm) diameter circle from this patchwork. Cut a 7-in. (17.8-cm) diameter circle from the centre of the A square. Insert the patchwork circle into the square (see piecing a circle, page 23).

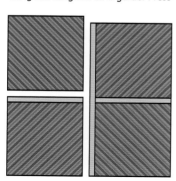

EMBROIDERY
Embroider three lazy daisy stitches at the end of each C strip (page 27).

Construction

Cut the B pieces with the striped fabric on the bias. Sew one B piece to each of the corner A pieces (see piecing curves, page 23). Press the seams towards B. Sew the corner units to the centre A piece, attaching opposite corners in pairs. Press the seams towards the corners.

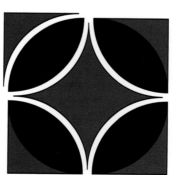

64 Chū kage shippō
(Shaded centre seven treasures)

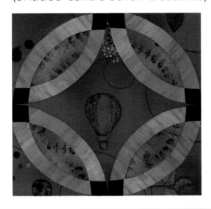

Inspired by ancient
Japanese court designs.

A

B

C

D

CUTTING LIST

A   One piece from template 63a (page 113).
A   Four pieces from template 63b (page 115).
B   Four pieces from template 64a (page 113).
C   Eight pieces from template 64b (page 113).
D   Eight pieces from template 64c (page 113).

65 Ōoka shippō
(Great seven treasures)

Inspired by geometric
kamon (family crests).

A

B

C

D

CUTTING LIST

A   One 9½ in. (24 cm) square.
A   One piece from template 65a (page 110).
B   Four pieces from template 65b (page 114).
C   Eight pieces from template 65c (page 114).
D   Eight pieces from template 65d (page 112).

Construction

Sew each B piece to one C piece (see piecing curves, page 23). Press the seams towards B. Sew one D piece to each end of the remaining C pieces. Press the seams towards D. Sew one C/D unit to each C/B unit to complete the corner units. Press the seams towards B. Sew the corner units to the centre A piece, attaching opposite corners in pairs. Press the seams towards the corners.

Construction

Sew all the B pieces to the centre A piece (see piecing curves, page 23). Press the seams towards B. Sew each C piece to one D piece, then sew all the C/D units together to make a ring. Press the seams towards C. Cut a 7-in. (17.8-cm) diameter circle from the centre of the A square. Insert the C/D ring into the square, then insert the centre A/B unit into the ring (see piecing a circle, page 23). Press the seams outwards.

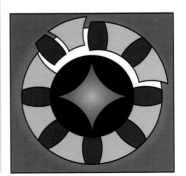

66 Tatewaku
(Rising steam)

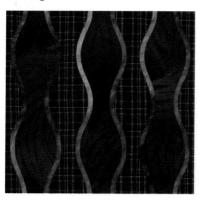

Inspired by ancient
Japanese court designs.

CUTTING LIST

A   One 9½ in. (24 cm) square.

B   Three pieces from template 66 (page 116);
do not add turning allowances.
About 2 yds (1.8 m) of ¼ in. (6 mm) fusible bias tape.

Construction

Mark a vertical line at the centre of the A square, then another vertical line 3 in. (7.6 cm) to the left and to the right. Line up the centre of the B pieces on the lines. Sew to the background, stitching ⅛ in. (3 mm) from the edges. Position and appliqué the bias tape so that it covers the edges of the B pieces. Refer to pages 24–25 for tips on appliqué.

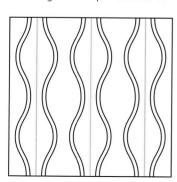

67 Seigaiha
(Ocean waves)

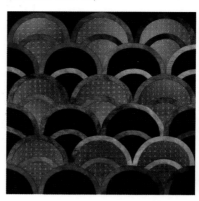

Inspired by traditional
Japanese patterns and
woven kimono fabrics.

CUTTING LIST

A   One 9½ in. (24 cm) square.

B   Nine pieces from template 67 (page 116);
do not add turning allowances.
About 2½ yds (2.3 m) of ¼ in. (6 mm) fusible bias tape.

Construction

Mark a ¼ in. (6 mm) seam allowance all around the A square, then mark a 1½ in. (3.8 cm) grid on the centre of the A square.

Line up the B pieces on the grid and then sew to the background, stitching ⅛ in. (3 mm) from the edges. Starting with the top row of arcs, position and appliqué the bias tape so that it covers the edges of the B pieces. Overlap the ends of the tape with subsequent rows of arcs. Refer to pages 24–25 for tips on appliqué.

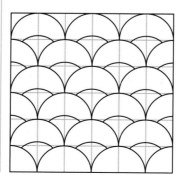

Project 3
Tote bag

Adding borders to two blocks makes them large enough for a handy tote bag. Appliqué blocks 66 and 67 were selected, which have no raw edges on the back, so quilting was not required (if you use patchwork blocks, you will need to quilt or back them). Try varying fabrics for the borders. The bag is 17 in. (43.2 cm) long and 15 in. (38.1 cm) wide.

REVERSE

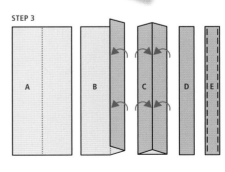

YOU WILL NEED

- Two blocks of your choice.
- Two 9½ x 3½ in. (24 x 8.9 cm) strips for top borders.
- Two 9½ x 5½ in. (24 x 14 cm) strips for bottom borders.
- Four 17½ x 3½ in. (44.5 x 8.9 cm) strips for side borders.
- Two 17½ x 15½ in. (44.5 x 39.4 cm) lining pieces.
- Two 13 x 4 in. (33 x 10.2 cm) strips for handles; if you want to adjust the handle dimensions, each strip should be four times the required finished width x the required finished length plus 1 in. (2.5 cm).

Construction

1 Arrange and sew the blocks and border strips to make the side panels. Zigzag the seams as you go, and press towards the outside.

2 Place the panels right sides together and machine sew the sides and base, starting and finishing with a few backstitches. Sew the lining pieces together in the same way, but leave a 4 in. (10.2 cm) gap in one side seam.

3 Fold and press each handle strip along the centre (A). Fold the long sides to the centre crease and press again (B). Fold the strip

STEP 1

in half along the centre (C). There will now be four layers of fabric, with the raw edges hidden in the centre (D). Machine sew along each edge (E). Secure the layers with one or two evenly spaced lines of stitching along the handle.

4 With the bag right side out, tack a handle to the centre of each panel, with a 3 in. (8.9 cm) gap between the ends of the handles. Allow the ends to protrude ½ in. (1.3 cm) above the panels. Insert the lining (page 101, step 5).

STEP 3

A   B   C   D   E

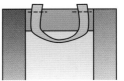

STEP 4

68 Mitsu kasane jigami
(Three layered fan papers)

Inspired by kamon (family crests) featuring plants, leaves and objects.

A
B
C
D

CUTTING LIST

A   One 9½ in. (24 cm) square.
B   One fan from template 68a (page 116).
C   One fan from template 68b (page 116).
D   One fan from template 68b (page 116).

Construction

Mark vertical and horizontal lines through the centre of the A square. Arrange and sew the block, using the diagram as a guide, overlapping the fan papers. Appliqué the largest fan paper last. Refer to pages 24–25 for tips on appliqué.

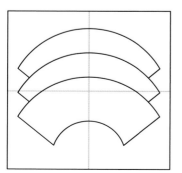

69 Kawari kazaguruma
(Windmill variation)

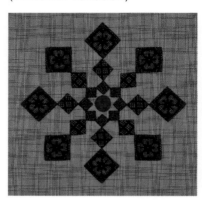

Inspired by kamon (family crests) featuring plants, leaves and objects.

A
B
C

CUTTING LIST

A   One 9½ in. (24 cm) square.
B   Eight 1¾ in. (4.4 cm) squares.
B   Eight 1¼ in. (3.2 cm) squares.
B   Eight 1 in. (2.5 cm) squares.
C   One 1-in. (2.5-cm) diameter circle.

Construction

Mark vertical, horizontal and diagonal lines through the centre of the A square. Press under a ¼ in. (6 mm) hem all around each B square. Arrange and sew the block, using the diagram as a guide, starting with the smallest B squares. Appliqué the circle to the block centre last. Refer to pages 24–25 for tips on appliqué.

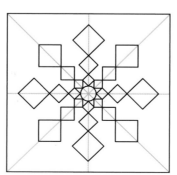

70 Shikishi
(Calligraphy cards)

Inspired by kamon (family crests) featuring plants, leaves and objects.

A
B
C

CUTTING LIST
A   One 9½ in. (24 cm) square.
B   Six 2⅞ x 2¾ in. (7.3 x 7 cm) pieces.
C   Six 2 in. (5 cm) squares.

Construction

Mark horizontal and 60-degree lines through the centre of the A square. Press under a ¼ in. (6 mm) hem all around each B piece. Do the same on three sides of each C piece; the remaining edges will be overlapped by the B pieces. Arrange and sew the block, using the diagram as a guide. The inner corners of the B pieces are ⅝ in. (1.6 cm) from the centre. Refer to pages 24–25 for tips on appliqué.

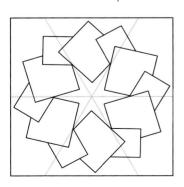

71 Mizuno kengata rokuyō
(Mizuno sword-shaped six leaves)

Inspired by kamon (family crests) featuring plants, leaves and objects.

A
B
C

CUTTING LIST
A   One 9½ in. (24 cm) square.
B   Six pieces from template 71 (page 117).
C   One 1½-in. (3.8-cm) diameter circle.

Construction

Mark vertical and 60-degree lines through the centre of the A square. Arrange and sew the block, using the diagram as a guide. Appliqué the circle to the block centre last. Refer to pages 24–25 for tips on appliqué.

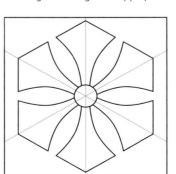

72 Itsutsu matsukawabishi
(Five pine bark diamonds)

Inspired by kamon (family crests) featuring plants, leaves and objects.

A

B

CUTTING LIST

A   One 9½ in. (24 cm) square.
B   Five pieces from template 72 (page 117).

Construction

Mark vertical and 72-degree lines radiating from the centre of the A square. Arrange and sew the block, using the diagram as a guide. Refer to pages 24–25 for tips on appliqué.

73 Yama fubuki
(Mountain snowstorm)

Inspired by kamon (family crests) featuring plants, leaves and objects.

A

B

CUTTING LIST

A   One 9½ in. (24 cm) square.
B   Six pieces from template 73 (page 117).

Construction

Mark vertical and 60-degree lines through the centre of the A square. Arrange and sew the block, using the diagram as a guide. Refer to pages 24–25 for tips on appliqué.

Yatsunazuna
(Shepherd's purse)

Inspired by kamon (family crests) featuring plants, leaves and objects.

Hoya no hana
(Hoya flower)

Inspired by kamon (family crests) featuring plants, leaves and objects.

A
B
C

CUTTING LIST

A   One 9½ in. (24 cm) square.
B   Eight leaves from template 74 (page 117).
C   One yoyo, about ⅝ in. (1.6 cm) diameter (page 26).

A
B
C
D

CUTTING LIST

A   One 9½ in. (24 cm) square.
B   Eight petals from template 75a (page 116).
C   Eight petals from template 75b (page 116).
D   One 1-in. (2.5-cm) diameter circle.

Construction

Mark vertical, horizontal and diagonal lines through the centre of the A square. Arrange and sew the block, using the diagram as a guide. Start with the vertical and horizontal leaves. Appliqué the yoyo to the block centre last. Refer to pages 24–25 for tips on appliqué.

EMBROIDERY
Embroider leaf veins in stem stitch (page 27).

Construction

Mark vertical, horizontal and diagonal lines through the centre of the A square. Mark 8-in. (20.3-cm) and 4½-in. (11.4-cm) diameter circles centred on the square. Arrange and sew the block, using the diagram as a guide. Start with the outer petals. Appliqué the circle to the block centre last. Refer to pages 24–25 for tips on appliqué.

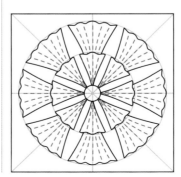

EMBROIDERY
Embroider petal details in stem stitch (page 27).

76 Kumai sasa kuruma
(Nine bamboo leaves wheel)

Inspired by kamon (family crests) featuring plants, leaves and objects.

A
B
C

CUTTING LIST

A   One 9½ in. (24 cm) square.
B   Nine pieces from template 76 (page 117).
C   One ¾-in. (1.9-cm) diameter circle.

Construction

Mark vertical and 40-degree lines radiating from the centre of the A square. Arrange and sew the block, using the diagram as a guide. Position the base of each leaf ¾ in. (1.9 cm) from the block centre. Appliqué the circle to the block centre last. Refer to pages 24–25 for tips on appliqué.

77 Ken yotsu me
(Four sword squares)

Inspired by kamon (family crests) featuring plants, leaves and objects.

A
B
C
D

CUTTING LIST

A   One 9½ in. (24 cm) square.
B   Four 2¼ in. (5.7 cm) squares.
C   Four pieces from template 77 (page 117).
D   One 1½-in. (3.8-cm) diameter circle.
Four 1½ in. (3.8 cm) pieces of ¼ in. (6 mm) fusible bias tape.

Construction

Mark vertical, horizontal and diagonal lines through the centre of the A square. Arrange and sew the block, using the diagram as a guide. Start with the template pieces. Press under a ¼ in. (6 mm) hem all around each B square. Position the B squares and bias tape, tucking the ends of the bias tape under the squares. Appliqué the circle to the block centre last. Refer to pages 24–25 for tips on appliqué.

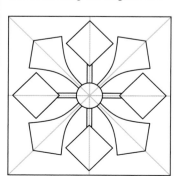

Project 4

Table runner

Symmetrical appliqué blocks in warm tones – 69, 71, 72, 73, 76 and 77 – were chosen for this table runner, but they have been set asymmetrically with patchwork sections. The patchwork strips can be identical, or you can use up fabric scraps. Make the runner as long as you like; this one is 64 in. (162.6 cm) long and 12 in. (30.5 cm) wide.

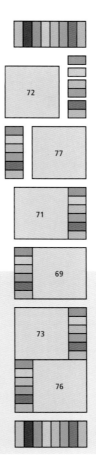

STEP 1

YOU WILL NEED

- Six blocks of your choice.
- Thirty-six 3½ x 2 in. (8.9 x 5 cm) strips (six each in assorted fabrics).
- Sixteen 5 x 2 in. (12.7 x 5c m) strips (two each in assorted fabrics).
- One 65 x 13 in. (165.1 x 33 cm) piece for backing.
- One 65 x 13 in. (165.1 x 33 cm) piece of wadding.

Construction

1 Arrange and sew the blocks and patchwork border. Press the seams towards the blocks.

2 Spread out the wadding and lay the backing piece wrong side down on top of it. Tack with stitches (pins tend to catch on each other when turning the quilt right side out). Lay the quilt top right side down onto the backing, and smooth it out. Pin and machine sew all around, leaving a gap unsewn at the bottom that will be big enough to turn the whole quilt through.

3 Trim the backing to match the quilt top. Trim the excess wadding from the seam allowance and across the gap. Clip the corners diagonally to about ⅛ in. (3 mm) from the edge and turn the quilt right side out through the unsewn gap – this is called 'bagging out'. Smooth the top over the wadding and backing, then tack the layers together.

4 Quilt the top panel. The patchwork borders on this table runner were machine quilted in zigzags, with contour quilting around the motifs on the blocks,

about ⅛ in. (3 mm) from the edges (page 30). Slipstitch the turning gap closed.

BAGGING OUT

This is a good method for small projects with no binding, but bagging out a very large quilt is tricky. Note that the layers of the quilt sandwich are tacked together in a different order than normal.

78 Rokuyō
(Hexagonal flower)

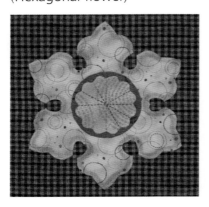

Inspired by kamon (family crests) featuring plants, leaves and objects.

A

B

C

D

CUTTING LIST

A   One 9½ in. (24 cm) square.
B   One piece from template 78a (page 118).
C   One 3½-in. (8.9-cm) diameter circle.
D   One flower from template 78b (page 118).

Construction

Mark vertical and horizontal lines through the centre of the A square. Arrange and sew the block, using the diagram as a guide. Start with the B piece. Refer to pages 24–25 for tips on appliqué.

EMBROIDERY
Embroider petal details in running stitch (page 27).

79 Mizuno rokuyō
(Mizuno hexagonal flower)

Inspired by kamon (family crests) featuring plants, leaves and objects.

A

B

C

D

CUTTING LIST

A   One 9½ in. (24 cm) square.
B   One piece from template 79a (page 118).
C   One piece from template 79b (page 118).
D   One flower from template 78b (page 118).

Construction

Mark vertical and horizontal lines through the centre of the A square. Arrange and sew the block, using the diagram as a guide. Start with the B piece. Refer to pages 24–25 for tips on appliqué.

EMBROIDERY
Embroider petal details in running stitch (page 27).

Neji nioi ume
(Matching twisted plum blossom)

Inspired by kamon (family crests) featuring plants, leaves and objects.

Hata guruma
(Flag wheel)

Inspired by kamon (family crests) featuring plants, leaves and objects.

CUTTING LIST

 A

 B

 C

A   One 9½ in. (24 cm) square.
B   Five petals from template 80 (page 118).
C   One yoyo, about 1 in. (2.5 cm) diameter (page 26).

CUTTING LIST

 A

 B

 C

A   One 9½ in. (24 cm) square.
B   Six 2¾ x 2½ in. (7 x 6.4 cm) pieces in assorted fabrics.
C   Six ⅞-in. (2.2-cm) diameter circles.
C   One 1-in. (2.5-cm) diameter circle.
Six 3½ in. (8.9 cm) pieces of ¼ in. (6 mm) fusible bias tape.

Construction

Mark vertical and 72-degree lines radiating from the centre of the A square. Arrange and sew the block, using the diagram as a guide. Overlap the B pieces. Appliqué the yoyo to the block centre last. Refer to pages 24–25 for tips on appliqué.

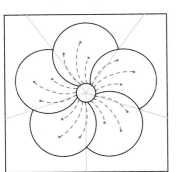

EMBROIDERY

Embroider petal details in running stitch; add a French knot at the end of each line of stitching (page 27).

Construction

Mark vertical and 60-degree lines through the centre of the A square. Press under a ¼ in. (6 mm) hem around three sides of each B piece; the remaining edges will be overlapped by the bias tape flagpoles. Arrange and sew the block, using the diagram as a guide. Appliqué the circles last. Refer to pages 24–25 for tips on appliqué.

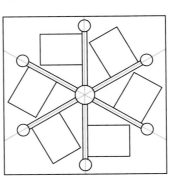

82 Kazaguruma
(Windmill)

Inspired by kamon (family crests) featuring plants, leaves and objects.

CUTTING LIST

A   A   One 9½ in. (24 cm) square.

B   B   Eight 2¼ in. (5.7 cm) squares.

      B   One 3-in. (7.6-cm) diameter circle, with a 2-in. (5-cm) diameter circle cut from the centre of it to make a ring.

      B   One 1¼-in. (3.2-cm) diameter circle.

      Eight 2¼ in. (5.7 cm) pieces of ¼ in. (6 mm) fusible bias tape.

Construction

Mark vertical, horizontal and diagonal lines through the centre of the A square. Press under a ¼ in. (6 mm) hem all around each B square. Arrange and sew the block, using the diagram as a guide. Appliqué the ring and circle to the block centre last. Refer to pages 24–25 for tips on appliqué.

83 Fudegata rinpō
(Brush-shaped treasure wheel)

Inspired by kamon (family crests) featuring plants, leaves and objects.

CUTTING LIST

A   A   One 9½ in. (24 cm) square.

B   B   Eight pieces from template 83a (page 117).

C   C   Eight pieces from template 83b (page 116).

D   D   Eight 1 x 1¾ in. (2.5 x 4.4 cm) strips.

E   E   One 1½-in. (3.8-cm) diameter circle.

Construction

Mark vertical, horizontal and diagonal lines through the centre of the A square. Press under a ¼ in. (6 mm) hem along each long side of the D strips; leave the short ends raw. Arrange and sew the block, using the diagram as a guide. Appliqué the circle to the block centre last. Refer to pages 24–25 for tips on appliqué.

84 Yamabuki
(Kerria rose)

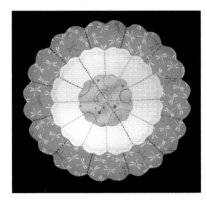

Inspired by kamon (family crests) featuring plants, leaves and objects.

CUTTING LIST

A — One 9½ in. (24 cm) square.
B — One piece from template 84a (page 119).
C — One piece from template 84b (page 119).
D — One piece from template 84c (page 119).

Construction

Mark horizontal and 60-degree lines through the centre of the A square. Arrange and sew the block, using the diagram as a guide. Appliqué the B piece first, followed by C and then D. Refer to pages 24–25 for tips on appliqué.

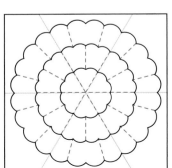

EMBROIDERY
Indicate individual petals in running stitch (page 27).

Mix & match
quilt designs

Diagonal divisions

▲ Block 5 makes a stepped base, with blocks 39 (repeated), 82, 83, 84 and 118 above.

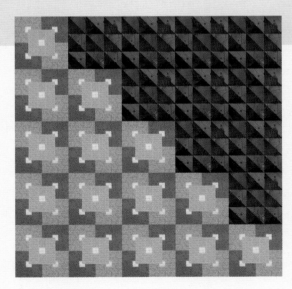

▲ Blocks 8 and 30 are arranged along a diagonal axis.

85

Hanakaku
(Flower square)

Inspired by kamon (family crests) featuring plants, leaves and objects.

CUTTING LIST

A
B
C
D

A   One 9½ in. (24 cm) square.
B   Two petals from template 85a (page 120).
B   Four petals from template 85b (page 119).
B   Four petals from template 85b flipped (page 119).
C   Two petals from template 85c (page 120).
C   Four petals from template 85d (page 119).
D   Four pieces from template 85e (page 119).
D   One yoyo, about 1 in. (2.5 cm) diameter (page 26).

Construction

Mark vertical and horizontal lines through the centre of the A square. Arrange and sew the block, using the diagram as a guide. Start with the B pieces. Gaps between B and C pieces should be ⅛ in. (3 mm). Appliqué the D pieces last. Refer to pages 24–25 for tips on appliqué.

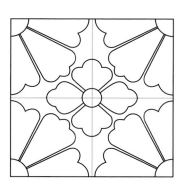

86

Sengoku kuyō sakura
(Nine cherry blossom enclosure)

Inspired by kamon (family crests) featuring plants, leaves and objects.

CUTTING LIST

A
B

A   One 9½ in. (24 cm) square.
B   Eight flowers from template 86a (page 120).
B   One flower from template 86b (page 121).

Construction

Mark vertical, horizontal and diagonal lines through the centre of the A square. Arrange and sew the block, using the diagram as a guide. Refer to pages 24–25 for tips on appliqué.

EMBROIDERY

Embroider flower centres in running stitch; end each line of stitching with a French knot for the larger flower (page 27).

87 Daki hagi
(Embracing bush clover)

Inspired by kamon (family crests) featuring plants, leaves and objects.

88 Tabane hagi
(Bush clover bundle)

Inspired by kamon (family crests) featuring plants, leaves and objects.

A
B

CUTTING LIST

A　One 9½ in. (24 cm) square.
B　Six leaves from template 87a (page 119).
B　Fourteen leaves from template 87b (page 119).
B　Eight leaves from template 87c (page 119).
Two 10 in. (25.4 cm), four 1½ in. (3.8 cm) and
four 1 in. (2.5 cm) pieces of ¼ in. (6 mm) fusible bias tape.

A
B

CUTTING LIST

A　One 9½ x 7¾ in. (24 x 19.7 cm) strip.
A　One 9½ x 2¼ in. (24 x 5.7 cm) strip.
B　Seventeen leaves from template 87b (page 119).
One 6½ in. (16.5 cm), two 7 in. (17.8 cm), two 5½ in. (14 cm)
and two 3½ in. (8.9 cm) pieces of ¼ in. (6 mm) fusible bias tape.

Construction

Mark vertical and horizontal lines through the centre of the A square. Mark the overlapping curves for the bias tape with a 7½-in. (19-cm) diameter circle template. Arrange and sew the block, using the diagram as a guide. Refer to pages 24–25 for tips on appliqué.

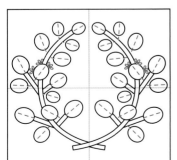

EMBROIDERY
Embroider leaf details in stem stitch; add flowers in lazy daisy stitch (page 27).

ALTERNATIVE DESIGN
Use tiny buttons for flowers.

Construction

Mark a vertical line through the centre of the larger A strip. Arrange and sew the block, using the diagram as a guide. All bias tape should reach the bottom edge of the strip. Refer to pages 24–25 for tips on appliqué. Sew the smaller A strip to the base to complete the block.

EMBROIDERY
Embroider leaf details in stem stitch; add flowers in lazy daisy stitch (page 27).

ALTERNATIVE DESIGN
Use tiny buttons for flowers.

89 Kumori yuki
(Cloudy snow)

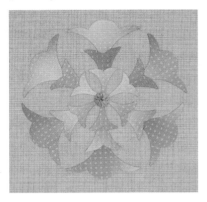

Inspired by kamon (family crests) featuring plants, leaves and objects.

A

B

CUTTING LIST

A   One 9½ in. (24 cm) square.
B   Six pieces from template 89a (page 120).
B   Six pieces from template 89b (page 120).
B   Six pieces from template 89c (page 120).
B   One yoyo, about ⅝ in. (1.6 cm) diameter (page 26).

Construction

Mark vertical and 60-degree lines through the centre of the A square. Mark an 8-in. (20.3-cm) diameter circle centred on the square, to line up the outer pieces. Arrange and sew the block, using the diagram as a guide. Start with outer pieces. Appliqué the yoyo to the block centre last. Refer to pages 24–25 for tips on appliqué.

90 Yayuki
(Snow arrow)

Inspired by kamon (family crests) featuring plants, leaves and objects.

A

B

CUTTING LIST

A   One 9½ in. (24 cm) square.
B   Six pieces from template 90a (page 120).
B   Twelve pieces from template 90b (page 120).
B   Twelve pieces from template 90c (page 120).
B   Twelve pieces from template 90d (page 120).
B   One yoyo, about 1½ in. (3.8 cm) diameter (page 26).
Six 3¼ in. (8.3 cm) pieces of ¼ in. (6 mm) fusible bias tape.

Construction

Mark vertical and 60-degree lines through the centre of the A square. Arrange and sew the block, using the diagram as a guide. Overlap the outer ends of the bias tape with the heart shapes. Appliqué the yoyo to the block centre last, overlapping the inner ends of the bias tape. Refer to pages 24–25 for tips on appliqué.

91 Tsurura yuki
(Snow icicles)

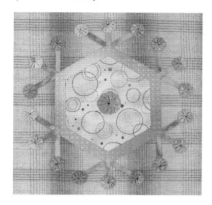

Inspired by kamon (family crests) featuring plants, leaves and objects.

A

B

CUTTING LIST

A   One 9½ in. (24 cm) square.
B   One hexagon frame from template 91a (page 120).
B   Eighteen yoyos, about ⅝ in. (1.6 cm) diameter (page 26).
B   One yoyo, about 1 in. (2.5 cm) diameter.
C   One hexagon from template 91b (page 121).
Eighteen 1⅝ in. (4.1 cm) pieces of ¼ in. (6 mm) fusible bias tape.

92 Kiri no hana guruma
(Paulownia flower wheel)

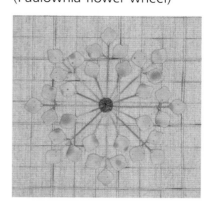

Inspired by kamon (family crests) featuring plants, leaves and objects.

A

B

C

CUTTING LIST

A   One 9½ in. (24 cm) square.
B   Thirty-two flowers from template 92 (page 120).
C   One yoyo, about ⅝ in. (1.6 cm) diameter (page 26).

Construction

Mark vertical and 60-degree lines through the centre of the A square. Arrange and sew the block, using the diagram as a guide. Centre the

C hexagon and align the bias tape. Appliqué the B hexagon frame to cover the raw edges. Appliqué the yoyos last. Refer to pages 24–25 for tips on appliqué.

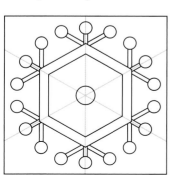

Construction

Mark 22.5-degree lines through the centre of the A square. Arrange and sew the block, using the diagram as a guide. Appliqué

the yoyo to the block centre last. Refer to pages 24–25 for tips on appliqué.

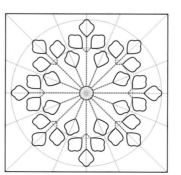

EMBROIDERY

Embroider flower stems in chain stitch, with a fly stitch connecting the chains to the flowers (page 27).

ALTERNATIVE DESIGN

Substitute the flower appliqués with flower-shaped buttons.

93 Hosoneji kiri guruma
(Elongated paulownia wheel)

Inspired by kamon (family crests) featuring plants, leaves and objects.

A
B
C
D

CUTTING LIST

A   One 9½ in. (24 cm) square.
B   Five leaves from template 93 (page 121).
C   Fifteen flowers from template 92 (page 120).
D   One yoyo, about 1 in. (2.5 cm) diameter (page 26).

Construction

Mark 72-degree lines radiating from the centre of the A square. Arrange and sew the block, using the diagram as a guide. Appliqué the yoyo to the block centre last. Refer to pages 24–25 for tips on appliqué.

EMBROIDERY
Embroider flower stems in chain stitch, with a fly stitch connecting the chains to the flowers; embroider leaf veins in stem stitch (page 27).

ALTERNATIVE DESIGN
Substitute the flower appliqués with flower-shaped buttons.

94 Kikkō guruma
(Bellflower wheel)

Inspired by kamon (family crests) featuring plants, leaves and objects.

A
B
C
D

CUTTING LIST

A   One 9½ in. (24 cm) square.
B   Five flowers from template 94a (page 121).
C   Five leaves from template 94b (page 121).
D   One yoyo, about 1 in. (2.5 cm) diameter (page 26).
Five 2⅝ in. (6.7 cm) pieces of ¼ in. (6 mm) fusible bias tape.

Construction

Mark vertical and 36-degree lines radiating from the centre of the A square. Arrange and sew the block, using the diagram as a guide. Overlap the outer ends of the bias tape with flowers. Appliqué the yoyo to the block centre last, overlapping the inner ends of the bias tape. Refer to pages 24–25 for tips on appliqué.

EMBROIDERY
Embroider flower details and leaf veins in stem stitch (page 27).

95 Itadori
(Japanese knotweed)

Inspired by kamon (family crests) featuring plants, leaves and objects.

CUTTING LIST

A
B
C
D

A   One 9½ in. (24 cm) square.
B   Five leaves from template 95 (page 121).
C   Twenty-five yoyos, about ⅝ in. (1.6 cm) diameter (page 26).
D   One yoyo, about 1 in. (2.5 cm) diameter.
Five 3½ in. (8.9 cm), ten 1½ in. (3.8 cm) and ten ⅞ in. (2.2 cm) pieces of ¼ in. (6 mm) fusible bias tape.

Construction

Mark vertical and 36-degree lines through the centre of the A square. Arrange and sew the block, using the diagram as a guide. Appliqué the yoyos last, overlapping the ends of the bias tape. Refer to pages 24–25 for tips on appliqué.

EMBROIDERY
Embroider leaf veins in stem stitch (page 27).

ALTERNATIVE DESIGN
Embroider chain-stitch stems in place of the bias tape; substitute the smaller yoyos with flower-shaped buttons.

Mix & match
quilt designs

Sampler collection

▲ An arrangement of 35 individual blocks.

11	78	41	116	33
115	38	111	15	120
37	124	40	125	32
82	24	84	19	83
44	123	43	122	36
118	16	62	39	117
35	119	42	79	12

96 Tsuzumi
(Hand drum)

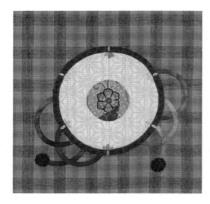

Inspired by kamon (family crests) featuring plants, leaves and objects.

A
B
C
D

CUTTING LIST

A One 9½ in. (24 cm) square.
B One 5-in. (12.7-cm) diameter circle.
C One 2½-in. (6.4-cm) diameter circle.
D One 5¾-in. (14.6-cm) diameter circle, with a 4¼-in. (10.8-cm) diameter circle cut from the centre of it to make a hoop.
D Two yoyos, about ⅝ in. (1.6 cm) diameter (page 26).
About 30 in. (76 cm) of ¼ in. (6 mm) fusible bias tape.

Construction

Mark vertical and horizontal lines through the centre of the A square. Arrange and sew the block, using the diagram as a guide. Appliqué the B circle without turning under a hem. Position and appliqué the bias tape, touching the edge of the B circle. Appliqué the D hoop to cover the ends of the bias tape and the B circle edge. Appliqué the C circle and yoyos last. Refer to pages 24–25 for tips on appliqué.

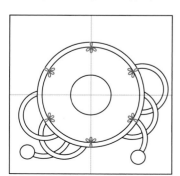

EMBROIDERY

Embroider groups of lazy daisy stitches around the hoop (page 27).

97 Nawa tsuki ikari
(Anchor with rope)

Inspired by kamon (family crests) featuring plants, leaves and objects.

A
B
C
D

CUTTING LIST

A One 9½ in. (24 cm) square.
B One piece from template 97a (page 122).
B One piece from template 97b (page 122).
B One piece from template 97b flipped (page 122).
B One 3 x 1 in. (7.6 x 2.5 cm) strip.
B One 1¼-in. (3.2-cm) diameter circle, with a ¾-in. (1.9-cm) diameter circle cut from the centre of it to make a hoop.
C Two yoyos, about ⅝ in. (1.6 cm) diameter (page 26).
D Two 1½ x 1 in. (3.8 x 2.5 cm) strips.
About 45 in. (115 cm) of ¼ in. (6 mm) fusible bias tape.

Construction

Mark vertical and horizontal lines through the centre of the A square. Mark an 8-in. (20.3-cm) diameter circle, centred on the A square.

Arrange and sew the block, using the diagram as a guide. Appliqué the template pieces first, leaving the top unsewn for the B hoop. Press under a ¼ in. (6 mm) hem all around the B strip and appliqué in place. Position and tack the hoop. Appliqué the bias tape and hoop. Press under a ¼ in. (6mm) hem all around the D strips. Appliqué the D strips and yoyos to form tassels. Refer to pages 24–25 for tips on appliqué.

98 Suzukiri
(Bells in Paulownia arrangement)

Inspired by kamon (family crests) featuring plants, leaves and objects.

CUTTING LIST

A   One 9½ in. (24 cm) square.

B   Three 3-in. (7.6-cm) diameter circles; cut a small slot in each circle, about ¼ x 2.5 in. (6 x 25 mm).

C   Three yoyos, about ⅝ in. (1.6 cm) diameter (page 26). About 30 in. (76 cm) of ¼ in. (6 mm) fusible bias tape.

Construction

Mark vertical and horizontal lines through the centre of the A square. Arrange and sew the block, using the diagram as a guide. Position and appliqué the loops of bias tape first. Iron the arcs of bias tape to the B circles before appliquéing the circles to the block. Refer to pages 24–25 for tips on appliqué.

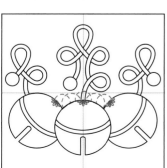

EMBROIDERY

Embroider groups of lazy daisy stitches at the top of each bell; use stem stitch to indicate rings (page 27).

99 Fusa tsuki uchiwa
(Tasselled moon fan)

Inspired by kamon (family crests) featuring plants, leaves and objects.

CUTTING LIST

A   One 9½ in. (24 cm) square.

B   One 6-in. (15.2-cm) diameter circle.

C   One piece from template 99 (page 121).

D   Two yoyos, about ⅝ in. (1.6 cm) diameter (page 26). About 30 in. (76 cm) of ¼ in. (6 mm) fusible bias tape.

Construction

Mark vertical and horizontal lines through the centre of the A square. Arrange and sew the block, using the diagram as a guide. Use 2-in. (5-cm) and 3½-in. (8.9-cm) diameter circle templates to position the lower left loops of tape, and a 2½ in. (6.4 cm) circle for the right loop. Refer to pages 24–25 for tips on appliqué.

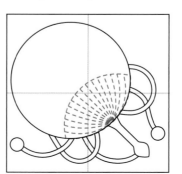

EMBROIDERY

Use a 5-in. (12.7-cm) diameter circle template to mark the outer arc of the fan ribs. Embroider the outer arc and the fan ribs in stem stitch (page 27).

100 Mittsu sakura no maru
(Triple cherry blossom circle)

Inspired by kamon (family crests) featuring plants, leaves and objects.

A

B

C

D

CUTTING LIST

A   One 9½ in. (24 cm) square.
B   One 7½-in. (19-cm) diameter circle.
C   Three flowers from template 86a (page 120).
D   Three leaves from template 100a (page 121).
D   Three leaves from template 100b (page 121).
D   Three leaves from template 100b flipped (page 121).
Three 12 in. (30.5 cm) pieces of ¼ in. (6 mm) fusible bias tape.

Construction

Mark horizontal and 60-degree lines through the centre of the A square. Arrange and sew the block, using the diagram as a guide. Appliqué the B circle without turning under a hem. Use the bias tape to cover the circle edge, tucking the start of each piece of tape under the previous piece at the edge of the circle. Refer to pages 24–25 for tips on appliqué.

EMBROIDERY
Embroider flower centres and leaf veins in running stitch (page 27).

101 Itsutsu tachi sakura
(Five cut cherry blossoms)

Inspired by kamon (family crests) featuring plants, leaves and objects.

A

B

C

CUTTING LIST

A   One 9½ x 7¾ in. (24 x 19.7 cm) strip.
A   One 9½ x 2¼ in. (24 x 5.7 cm) strip.
B   Five flowers from template 86a (page 120).
C   Six leaves from template 101 (page 122).
One 5¼ in. (13.3 cm), two 4¾ in. (12 cm) and two 2½ in. (6.4 cm) pieces of ¼ in. (6 mm) fusible bias tape.

Construction

Mark a vertical line through the centre of the larger A strip. Arrange and sew the block, using the diagram as a guide. Appliqué the longest piece of bias tape along the centre line first; the tape should reach the bottom edge of the strip. Appliqué a flower at the top of the tape. Appliqué the remaining tape, flowers and leaves. Refer to pages 24–25 for tips on appliqué. Sew the smaller A strip to the base to complete the block.

EMBROIDERY
Embroider the flower centres in running stitch (page 27).

Project 5
Wallhanging

Five appliqué blocks are arranged for a long, narrow hanging, reminiscent of the shape of a Japanese scroll. It is a good project to show off some of the more challenging blocks, such as 96, 97, 101, 107 and 112. Narrow sashing unites the blocks and separates them from the border. The wallhanging is 56 in. (142.2 cm) long and 14 in. (35.6 cm) wide.

YOU WILL NEED

- Five blocks of your choice.
- Six 9½ x 1 in. (24 x 2.5 cm) strips for sashing.
- Two 48½ x 1 in. (123.2 x 2.5 cm) strips for sashing.
- One 14½ x 3½ in. (36.8 x 8.9 cm) strip for top border.
- One 14½ x 5½ in. (36.8 x 14 cm) strip for bottom border.
- Two 48½ x 2½ in. (123.2 x 6.4 cm) strips for side borders.
- One 57 x 15 in. (144.8 x 38.1 cm) piece for backing.
- One 57 x 15 in. (144.8 x 38.1 cm) piece of wadding.
- One 14 x 4 in. (35.6 x 10.2 cm) strip for hanging sleeve.

STEP 1

Construction

1 Arrange and machine sew the front panel. Press the seams towards the border.

2 Following the instructions for bagging out (page 79, steps 2–3), layer the front panel, wadding and backing and turn right side out. Quilt the front panel. Here, the block edges, sashing and main appliqué motifs were machine quilted in the ditch (page 30). Slipstitch the turning gap closed.

3 Turn under a small hem at each end of the hanging sleeve strip. Fold the strip in half lengthways and machine sew to form a tube. Pin the top edge of the sleeve across the back of the quilt, about ½–¾ in. (1.3–1.9 cm) from the quilt top so that it will not show when hung. Position the sleeve seam on the inside so that it will not show. Hand sew the sleeve to the quilt backing (not through the front of the quilt).

4 Pin and sew the bottom edge of the sleeve to the quilt, rolling the edge up towards the top of the quilt by about ½ in. (1.3 cm), so that there is extra fullness across the outside of the sleeve to accommodate the hanging rod. The quilt will then hang without a bump across the top.

HANGING SLEEVE

102 Kani sakura
(Cherry blossom in crab arrangement)

Inspired by kamon (family crests) featuring plants, leaves and objects.

CUTTING LIST

A   One 9½ in. (24 cm) square.
B   One flower from template 86b (page 121).
B   Two flowers from template 102a (page 122).
B   One bud from template 102b (page 122)*.
C   One leaf each from templates 102c and 102d (page 122)*.
D   Two leaves from template 102d (page 122)*.
D   One leaf from template 102e (page 122)*.
Cut all pieces marked * again, templates flipped.
Two 3¾ in. (9.5 cm) and two 2 in. (5 cm) pieces of ¼ in. (6 mm) fusible bias tape.

Construction

Mark vertical and horizontal lines through the centre of the A square. Arrange and sew the block, using the diagram as a guide. Pin the large flower in place first. Leaves 102e link to 102c. Refer to pages 24–25 for tips on appliqué.

EMBROIDERY
Embroider the large flower centre in running stitch; end each line of stitching with a French knot. Embroider leaf veins in running stitch (page 27).

103 Daki kikyō
(Embracing bellflowers)

Inspired by kamon (family crests) featuring plants, leaves and objects.

CUTTING LIST

A   One 9½ in. (24 cm) square.
B   One flower from template 103a (page 122).
B   Two buds from template 103b (page 122).
C   Two leaves from template 103c (page 122).
C   Two leaves from template 103c flipped (page 122).
C   Four leaves from template 101 (page 122).
C   Two 1-in. (2.5-cm) diameter circles.
Two 4½ in. (11.4 cm), two 2⅞ in. (7.3 cm) and two 2 in. (5 cm) pieces of ¼ in. (6 mm) fusible bias tape.

Construction

Mark vertical and horizontal lines through the centre of the A square. Mark the overlapping curves for the bias tape with a 7½-in. (19-cm) diameter circle template. Arrange and sew the block, using the diagram as a guide. Use the longest pieces of bias tape for the lower curves; use the shortest pieces for the centre curves. Refer to pages 24–25 for tips on appliqué.

EMBROIDERY
Embroider flower and leaf details in stem stitch (page 27).

04 Hachi hon ōgi guruma
(Eight fan wheel)

Inspired by kamon (family crests) featuring plants, leaves and objects.

105 Nejigiku
(Twisted chrysanthemum)

Inspired by kamon (family crests) featuring plants, leaves and objects.

CUTTING LIST

A One 9½ in. (24 cm) square.
B Eight fans from template 104 (page 121) in assorted fabrics.
Eight 4½ in. (11.4 cm) pieces of ¼ in. (6 mm) fusible bias tape.

CUTTING LIST

A One 9½ in. (24 cm) square.
B Sixteen pieces from template 105 (page 122) in assorted fabrics.
C One yoyo, about 1 in. (2.5 cm) diameter (page 26).

Construction

Mark vertical, horizontal and diagonal lines through the centre of the A square. Iron a piece of bias tape down the centre of each fan; if using an appliqué method that requires hems, press under a hem along the narrow end of the fan before applying the bias tape. Arrange and sew the block, using the diagram as a guide. Refer to pages 24–25 for tips on appliqué.

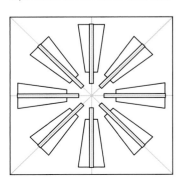

Construction

Mark 22.5-degree lines through the centre of the A square. Mark an 8-in. (20.3-cm) diameter circle centred on the square.

Arrange and sew the block, using the diagram as a guide. Overlap the petals so that the long edge of each petal hides the raw edge of the adjacent one. Appliqué the yoyo to the block centre last. Refer to pages 24–25 for tips on appliqué.

106 Ken giku
(Sword-petalled chrysanthemum)

Inspired by kamon (family crests) featuring plants, leaves and objects.

A
B
C

CUTTING LIST

A   One 9½ in. (24 cm) square.
B   Sixteen petals from template 106 (page 123), two each in assorted fabrics.
C   One yoyo, about 1 in. (2.5 cm) diameter (page 26).

Construction

Mark vertical and horizontal lines through the centre of the A square. Fold each petal in half lengthways, right sides together (1), and machine sew across the ends (2). Turn right side out and press to make the points (3). Sew petals together in pairs, then sew pairs together to make the flower. Press the seams open. Position and appliqué the flower to the A square. Appliqué the yoyo to the block centre last. Refer to pages 24–25 for tips on appliqué.

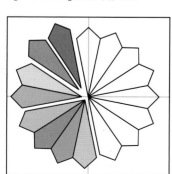

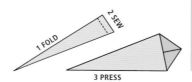

1 FOLD   2 SEW   3 PRESS

107 Jūgiku
(Ten petal chrysanthemum)

Inspired by kamon (family crests) featuring plants, leaves and objects.

A
B
C

CUTTING LIST

A   One 9½ in. (24 cm) square.
B   Ten pieces from template 107 (page 123) in assorted fabrics.
C   One 1¼-in. (3.2-cm) diameter circle.

Construction

Mark vertical and horizontal lines through the centre of the A square. Arrange and sew the block, using the diagram as a guide. Sewing as far as the dots on the template, sew the petals together in pairs, then sew the pairs together to make the flower. Position and appliqué the flower to the A square. Appliqué the circle to the block centre last. Refer to pages 24–25 for tips on appliqué.

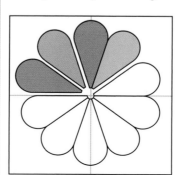

EMBROIDERY
Embroider the flower centre with five lazy daisy stitches (page 27).

Oni giku
(Jagged chrysanthemum)

Inspired by kamon (family crests) featuring plants, leaves and objects.

A

B

C

CUTTING LIST

A   One 9½ in. (24 cm) square.

B   Sixteen petals from template 108 (page 123), two each in assorted fabrics.

C   One yoyo, about 1 in. (2.5 cm) diameter (page 26).

Construction

Mark vertical and horizontal lines through the centre of the A square. Arrange and sew the block, using the diagram as a guide. Sewing as far as the dots on the template, sew the petals together in pairs, then sew the pairs together to make the flower. Position and appliqué the flower to the A square. Appliqué the yoyo to the block centre last. Refer to pages 24–25 for tips on appliqué.

Mix & match
quilt designs

Sampler collections

▲ Block 22 alternates with (from top left) blocks 105, 89, 108, 81, 112, 103, 75, 86, 97, 99, 106, 100 and 109.

▲ Blocks in cool shades (from top left): 26, 28, 51, 54, 9, 49, 55, 8, 64, 47, 7, 13, 59, 48, 3, 50, 52, 65, 61, 1, 53, 58, 30, 29 and 14.

109 Asa no hana
(Morning flower)

Inspired by kamon (family crests) featuring plants, leaves and objects.

CUTTING LIST

A   One 9½ in. (24 cm) square.

B   Sixteen 3¾ x 1½ in. (9.5 x 3.8 cm) strips, two each in assorted fabrics.

C   One yoyo, about 1 in. (2.5 cm) diameter (page 26).

110 Matsu guruma
(Pine wheel)

Inspired by kamon (family crests) featuring plants, leaves and objects.

CUTTING LIST

   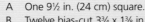 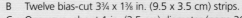

A   One 9½ in. (24 cm) square.

B   Twelve bias-cut 3¾ x 1⅜ in. (9.5 x 3.5 cm) strips.

C   One yoyo, about 1 in. (2.5 cm) diameter (page 26).

Six 4⅜ in. (11.1 cm) pieces of ¼ in. (6 mm) fusible bias tape.

Construction

Mark vertical and horizontal lines through the centre of the A square. Arrange and sew the block, using the diagram as a guide. With a

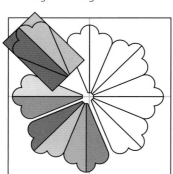

¼ in. (6 mm) seam, sew the B strips together in pairs. Press the seams open. Using template 109 (page 123), cut eight petals from the B strips, with the seam down the centre. Sewing as far as the dots on template, sew the petals together in pairs, then sew the pairs together to make the flower. Position and appliqué the flower to the A square. Appliqué the yoyo to the block centre last. Refer to pages 24–25 for tips on appliqué.

Construction

Mark vertical and 60-degree lines through the centre of the A square. Arrange and sew the block, using the diagram as a guide. Sew the

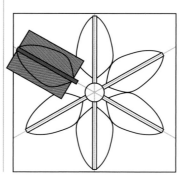

B strips together in pairs, arranging the stripes as shown in the photograph. Press the seams open. Using template 110 (page 123), cut six pine branches from the B strips, with the seam down the centre. Iron bias tape along each branch before appliquéing to the A square, tucking in the tape at the outer ends of the branches. Appliqué the yoyo to the block centre last. Refer to pages 24–25 for tips on appliqué.

111 Sumi no kirikuchi
(Inked sections)

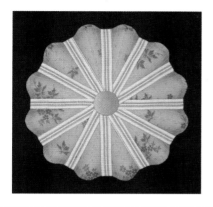

Inspired by kamon (family crests) featuring plants, leaves and objects.

112 Ōgi otoshi
(Upright fan)

Inspired by kamon (family crests) featuring plants, leaves and objects.

CUTTING LIST

A   One 9½ in. (24 cm) square.
B   Twelve petals from template 111 (page 123).
C   Twelve 3⅜ x 1 in. (8.6 x 2.5 cm) strips.
D   One 1½-in. (3.8-cm) diameter circle.

A
B
C
D

CUTTING LIST

A   One 9½ in. (24 cm) square.
B   One fan from template 112a (page 124).
C   One piece from template 112b (page 124).
C   One piece from template 112c (page 124).
C   One piece from template 112c flipped (page 124).
C   One 4½ x 2¾ in. (11.4 x 7 cm) strip.
D   Two 1½ x 1 in. (3.8 x 2.5 cm) strips.
E   Two yoyos, about ⅝ in. (1.6 cm) diameter (page 26).
Three 4½ in. (11.4 cm), three 3½ in. (8.9 cm) and four 2½ in. (6.4 cm) pieces of ¼ in. (6 mm) fusible bias tape.

Construction

Mark vertical and horizontal lines through the centre of the A square. Arrange and sew the block, using the diagram as a guide. Sew one

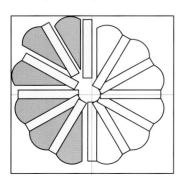

C strip to each petal, then sew these units together to make the flower. Press the seams towards the strips. Position and appliqué the flower to the A square. Appliqué the centre circle last. Refer to pages 24–25 for tips on appliqué.

Construction

Mark vertical and horizontal lines through the centre of the A square. Arrange and sew the block, using the diagram as a guide. Using a

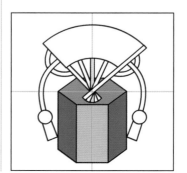

¼ in. (6 mm) allowance and inset seams (page 22), sew the C pieces together to form the hexagonal box. Turn under a ¼ in. (6 mm) hem all around the box and appliqué in place. Appliqué the fan, cords and sticks, tucking the cords and sticks under the fan; position the stick at the right edge over the fan. Finish the ends of the cords like tassels, turning under a ¼ in. (6mm) hem on the E strips and adding a yoyo. Refer to pages 24–25 for tips on appliqué.

113 Tessen
(Chinese clematis)

Inspired by kamon (family crests) featuring plants, leaves and objects.

A

B

C

D

E

CUTTING LIST

A   One 9½ in. (24 cm) square.
B   One 8 in. (20.3 cm) square.
C   One flower from template 113a (page 125).
D   One flower from template 113b (page 125).
E   One 1-in. (2.5-cm) diameter circle.

Construction

Mark vertical and horizontal lines through the centre of the B square. Arrange and sew the flower, starting with the C piece. Refer to pages 24–25 for tips on appliqué. Trim the B square to an 8-in. (20.3-cm) diameter circle. Cut a 7-in. (17.8-cm) diameter circle from the centre of the A square. Insert the pieced flower unit into the A square (see piecing a circle, page 23).

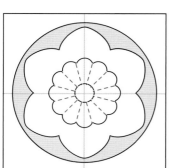

EMBROIDERY
Embroider petal details on the flower centre in running stitch (page 27).

114 Kikuha
(Chrysanthemum circle)

Inspired by kamon (family crests) featuring plants, leaves and objects.

A

B

CUTTING LIST

A   One 9½ in. (24 cm) square.
B   One 6-in. (15.2-cm) diameter circle.
C   Sixteen petals from template 114 (page 123).

Construction

Mark vertical, horizontal and diagonal lines through the centre of the A square. Mark a 5-in. (12.7-cm) diameter circle centred on the square. Appliqué the petals to the square, aligned around the marked circle. Refer to pages 24–25 for tips on appliqué. Cut out a 5-in. (12.7-cm) diameter circle from the centre of the square. Insert the B circle into the square (see piecing a circle, page 23).

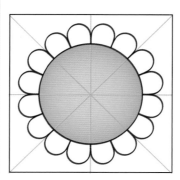

Project 6
Satchel bag

Three coordinated blocks – 2 (front), 6 (back) and 113 (flap) – were combined for this bag. Use this project to showcase a favourite block as the bag flap. Although it looks more complex, the basic construction method is similar to the tote bag on page 73. The bag measures about 9 in. (22.9 cm) high, 9 in. (22.9 cm) wide and 3 in. (8.9 cm) deep at the base.

BACK

YOU WILL NEED

- Three blocks of your choice.
- Three 10 in. (25.4 cm) squares of backing.
- Three 10 in. (25.4 cm) squares of wadding.
- One 3½ x 23¼ in. (8.9 x 59 cm) strip for gusset.
- Two 1½ x 2 in. (3.8 x 5 cm) strips for gusset tops.
- One 6 x 40 in. (15.2 x 101.6 cm) strip for strap.
- One 3½ x 23¼ in. (8.9 x 59 cm) strip for gusset lining.
- Two 1½ x 2 in. (3.8 x 5 cm) strips for gusset top linings.
- Three 9½ in. (24 cm) squares for panel lining.
- One large press-stud fastener (optional).

Construction

1 Layer and quilt the three blocks, wadding and backing squares. These blocks were machine quilted in the ditch, along seam lines and around motifs (page 30). Trim the wadding and backing to match the block edges. Use a 3½ in. (8.9 cm) circle template to curve the bottom corners of each block and panel lining piece. Overlock all around, or use a straight stitch and then a zigzag.

2 Place the bag flap right sides together with one panel lining square. Machine sew the sides and base. Turn the flap right side out through the unsewn top and press. Tack across the top. Make the strap (page 73, step 3).

3 Fold a box pleat at each end of the gusset, so that it fits to the long side of each gusset top strip, and machine sew. Repeat with the gusset lining pieces. Pin and sew the gusset to the front panel. Align the ends first and ease the gusset tightly around the curves, clipping the curves as necessary. Repeat with the back panel. Assemble the bag lining in the same way, leaving a 4 in. (10.2 cm) gap in one side seam.

4 Right sides together, pin and tack the bag flap to the top of the back panel and the strap to the top of the gusset, with the strap ends protruding ½ in. (1.3 cm) above the gusset.

5 With the bag right side out and the lining wrong side out, place the bag inside the lining. Machine sew around the top of the bag and lining using a ¼ in. (6 mm) seam. Turn right side out through the gap in the lining and press the seam. Sew around the top of the bag, about ⅛ in. (3 mm) from the edge. Turn the bag inside out

and slipstitch the lining gap closed. Sew the press stud to the bag front and under the flap.

GUSSET BOX PLEAT

115 Nabeshima hiashi
(Nabeshima sun)

Inspired by kamon (family crests) featuring plants, leaves and objects.

A

B

C

CUTTING LIST

A One 9½ in. (24 cm) square.
B One 8 in. (20.3 cm) square.
C One 1¾-in. (4.4-cm) diameter circle.
Twelve 3½ in. (8.9 cm) pieces of ¼ in. (6 mm) fusible bias tape.

Construction

Mark 30-degree lines through the centre of the B square, then mark an 8-in. (20.3-cm) diameter circle centred on the square. Iron and

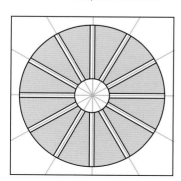

appliqué a piece of bias tape along each line, starting from the circle edge. Appliqué the C circle to the centre. Refer to pages 24–25 for tips on appliqué. Trim the B square to an 8-in. (20.3-cm) diameter circle. Cut a 7-in. (17.8-cm) diameter circle from the centre of the A square. Insert the pieced circle into the A square (see piecing a circle, page 23).

116 Ōgiwa
(Fan wheel)

Inspired by kamon (family crests) featuring plants, leaves and objects.

A

B

C

CUTTING LIST

A One 9½ in. (24 cm) square.
B One 4½-in. (11.4-cm) diameter circle.
B One 2¾-in. (7-cm) diameter circle.
C Sixteen fans from template 116 (page 124), four each in assorted fabrics.
Sixteen 2¾ in. (7 cm) pieces of ¼ in. (6 mm) fusible bias tape.

Construction

Mark vertical and horizontal lines through the centre of the A square. Sew the fans together in pairs, then sew the pairs together to make a

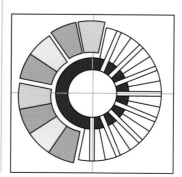

ring. Press the seams to one side. Insert the larger B circle into the ring (see piecing a circle, page 23). Mark lines radiating from the centre of the circle, along the centre of each fan. Iron and appliqué bias tape along each line. Refer to pages 24–25 for tips on appliqué. Cut a 7-in. (17.8-cm) diameter circle from the centre of the A square. Insert the fan circle into the A square. Appliqué the smaller B circle to the block centre last.

117 Jūni hiashi
(Twelve-rayed sun)

Inspired by kamon (family crests) featuring plants, leaves and objects.

A

B

CUTTING LIST

A   One 9½ in. (24 cm) square.
A   Twelve 3 x 1 in. (7.6 x 2.5 cm) strips.
B   Twelve sunrays from template 117 (page 124).
B   One 2¾-in. (7-cm) diameter circle.

Construction

Mark vertical and horizontal lines through the centre of the A square. Sew one A strip to each sunray, then sew the units together to make a circle. Press the seams towards the strips. Cut a 7-in. (17.8-cm) diameter circle from the centre of the A square. Insert the pieced circle into the A square (see piecing a circle, page 23). Appliqué the small B circle to the block centre. Refer to pages 24–25 for tips on appliqué.

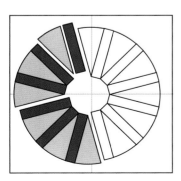

118 Karamatsu sensu
(Larch fan)

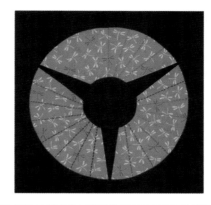

Inspired by kamon (family crests) featuring plants, leaves and objects.

A

B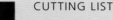

CUTTING LIST

A   One 9½ in. (24 cm) square.
A   Three pieces from template 118b (page 125).
A   One 2¾-in. (7-cm) diameter circle.
B   Three fans from template 118a (page 125).

Construction

Mark a vertical line through the centre of the A square. Sew one 118a piece to each fan piece, then sew the units together to make a circle. Press the seams towards the fans. Cut a 7-in. (17.8-cm) diameter circle from the centre of the A square. Insert the pieced fan circle into the A square (see piecing a circle, page 23). Appliqué the small A circle to the block centre. Refer to pages 24–25 for tips on appliqué.

EMBROIDERY
Embroider the fan details in running stitch (page 27).

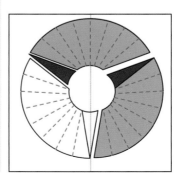

119 Muttsu ōgi
(Six fans)

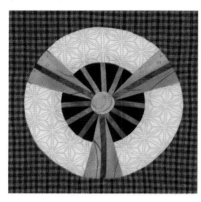

Inspired by kamon (family crests) featuring plants, leaves and objects.

120 Sasa guruma
(Bamboo wheel)

Inspired by kamon (family crests) featuring plants, leaves and objects.

A

B

C

D

E

CUTTING LIST

A   One 9½ in. (24 cm) square.
B   Three fans from template 119a (page 126).
C   Three fans from template 119b (page 126).
D   Three pieces from template 119c (page 126).
E   One 1¼-in. (3.2-cm) diameter circle.
Three 4 in. (10.2 cm) and nine 2 in. (5 cm) pieces of ¼ in. (6 mm) fusible bias tape.

A

B

C

D

CUTTING LIST

A   One 9½ in. (24 cm) square.
B   One 8 in. (20.3 cm) square.
C   Five leaves from template 120 (page 126).
D   One 1¼-in. (3.2-cm) diameter circle.
About 60 in. (153 cm) of ¼ in. (6 mm) fusible bias tape.

Construction

Mark a vertical line through the centre of the A square. Appliqué three small pieces of bias tape to each D piece, and one long piece of tape along the centre of each C fan. Sew each B fan to one C fan, then sew the units together with the D pieces to make a circle. Press the seams towards the B fans. Cut a 7-in. (17.8-cm) diameter circle from the centre of the A square. Insert the pieced fan circle into the A square (see piecing a circle, page 23). Appliqué the E circle to the block centre. Refer to pages 24–25 for tips on appliqué.

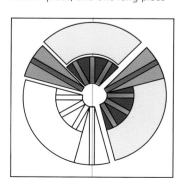

Construction

Mark 36-degree lines through the centre of the B square, then mark an 8-in. (20.3-cm) diameter circle centred on the square. Arrange and appliqué the leaves. Position and appliqué the bias tape as indicated on the diagram, starting with the shortest pieces. Appliqué the D circle to the centre. Refer to pages 24–25 for tips on appliqué. Trim the B square to an 8-in. (20.3-cm) diameter circle. Cut a 7-in. (17.8-cm) diameter circle from the centre of the A square. Insert the pieced circle into the square (see piecing a circle, page 23).

121 Kaku kuyō
(Nine squares)

Inspired by geometric kamon (family crests).

122 Dainichi rinpō
(Supreme Buddha treasure circle)

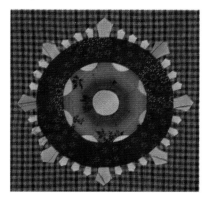

Inspired by kamon (family crests) featuring plants, leaves and objects.

CUTTING LIST

A Five 3½ in. (8.9 cm) squares.
B Four 3½ in. (8.9 cm) squares.
C One 2½-in. (6.4-cm) diameter circle.
D Two 2½-in. (6.4-cm) diameter circles.
E Two 2½-in. (6.4-cm) diameter circles.

CUTTING LIST

A One 9½ in. (24 cm) square.
B One 7-in. (17.8-cm) diameter circle.
C One 4½ in. (11.4 cm) square.
D Eight pieces from template 122a (page 124).
E Eight pieces from template 122b (page 124).
F Twenty-four pieces from template 122c (page 124).

Construction

Arrange and sew the block, using the diagram as a guide. Position and appliqué the circles to the A squares. Refer to pages 24–25 for tips on appliqué. Sew the pieces together into strips, then sew the strips together to complete block.

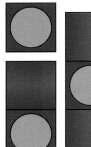
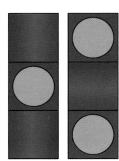

Construction

Sew the D pieces together in pairs, then sew the pairs together to make a ring. Mark a 4½-in. (11.4-cm) diameter circle on the C square. Appliqué the pieced D unit to the C square and trim to a circle. Mark vertical, horizontal and diagonal lines plus a 6-in. (15.2-cm) diameter circle on the A square. Appliqué the E and F pieces around the circle on the A square, then cut out the circle. Refer to pages 24–25 for tips on appliqué. Insert the B circle into the A square (see piecing a circle, page 23). Cut out a 3½-in. (8.9-cm) diameter circle from block centre and insert the C/D unit.

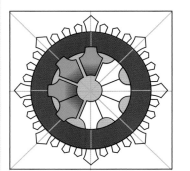

123 Narita rinpō
(Narita treasure wheel)

Inspired by kamon (family crests) featuring plants, leaves and objects.

A

B

C

D

CUTTING LIST

A   One 9½ in. (24 cm) square.
B   One 5½-in. (14-cm) diameter circle.
C   One flower from template 123a (page 126).
D   Eight pieces from template 123b (page 126).

Construction

Mark the A square with vertical, horizontal and diagonal lines plus a 4½-in. (11.4-cm) diameter circle. Appliqué the C flower to the centre and the D pieces around the circle. Cut out the circle. On the cutout piece, mark and cut out a 4 in. (10.2 cm) circle around the flower appliqué. Insert the B circle into the A square (see piecing a circle, page 23). Cut out a 3 in. (7.6 cm) circle from the block centre and insert the circular flower unit.

EMBROIDERY
Embroider petal details on the flower in running stitch (page 27).

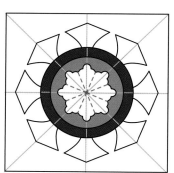

124 Takemono rinpō
(Bamboo treasure circle)

Inspired by kamon (family crests) featuring plants, leaves and objects.

A

B

C

D

E

CUTTING LIST

A   One 9½ in. (24 cm) square.
B   One 6½-in. (16.5-cm) diameter circle.
C   Eight pieces from template 124 (page 126).
D   Eight pieces from template 122b (page 124).
E   Twenty-four pieces from template 122c (page 124).

Construction

Mark the A square with vertical, horizontal and diagonal lines plus a 5½-in. (14-cm) diameter circle. Sew the C pieces together in pairs, then sew the pairs together to make a rosette. Appliqué the rosette to the centre of the A square. Appliqué the D and E pieces around the marked circle. Refer to pages 24–25 for tips on appliqué. Cut out the marked circle from the block. On the cutout piece, mark and cut out a 5 in. (12.7 cm) circle around the rosette appliqué. Insert the B circle into the A square (see piecing a circle, page 23). Cut out a 4 in. (10.2 cm) circle from the block centre and insert the circular rosette unit.

25 Kanō rinpō
(Kanō treasure wheel)

Inspired by kamon (family crests) featuring plants, leaves and objects.

A
B
C
D

CUTTING LIST

A One 9½ in. (24 cm) square.
B One 7-in. (17.8-cm) diameter circle.
C Eight petals from template 125a (page 126).
D Eight pieces from template 125b (page 126).

Construction

Mark the A square with vertical, horizontal and diagonal lines plus 6-in. (15.2-cm) and 4½-in. (11.4-cm) diameter circles. Appliqué the C petals around the inner circle and the D pieces around the outer circle. Refer to pages 24–25 for tips on appliqué. Cut out the larger circle. On the cutout piece, mark and cut out a 5 in. (12.7 cm) circle around the petal appliqué. Insert the B circle into the A square (see piecing a circle, page 23). Cut out a 4 in. (10.2 cm) circle from the block centre and insert the circular petal unit.

Mix & match
quilt designs

Frames or medallions with single centres

▲ Central block 83 is framed by blocks 122, 123, 124 and 125 alternated with block 39. Blocks 39 and 43 alternate around the edge.

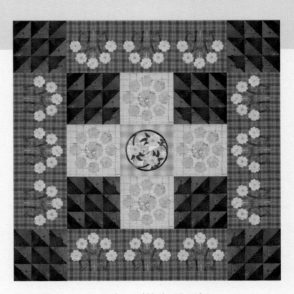

▲ Block 86 repeats around central block 100, with rotated block 8 cornerstones and block 101 borders.

Templates

The templates on pages 108–115 are for

patchwork blocks 1–65.

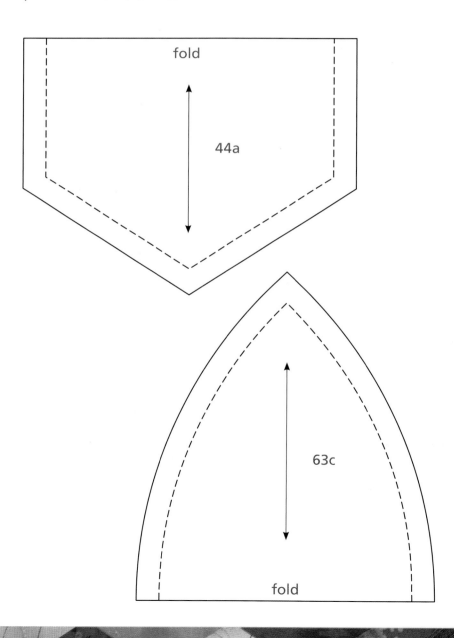

Using the templates

- The template reference number and page number are given in the block cutting list. A few templates are used in more than one block; the reference number relates to the first block where they are used.

- The templates are divided into the three categories of the block directory – patchwork, appliqué and combined technique – but note that they are not shown in precise block order here, due to space constraints.

- All of the templates are shown actual size. However, due to limited space, some of the templates need to be cut from paper folded in half or in quarters. All folds are clearly indicated.

- Trace or photocopy the templates you need for the block. Pin the templates to the fabric. A double-headed arrow on the template shows the direction of the fabric grain where it is important. Draw around the edge of the paper with a contrasting fabric marker or pencil. Cut out the pieces. Straight-edged pieces can be cut with a ruler and rotary cutter.

- All patchwork templates have a ¼ in. (6 mm) seam allowance already added, except for templates 107, 108 and 109, which have an ⅛ in. (3 mm) seam allowance on the curves only. The solid black line indicates the cutting line; the dashed black line within indicates the sewing line.

- The appliqué method you choose (pages 24–25) will dictate whether you need to add turning allowances when cutting out appliqué pieces. If using the fused appliqué method, do not add turning allowances; if using freezer paper appliqué, add ¼ in. (6 mm) allowances; if using needle-turn appliqué, add ⅛ in. (3 mm) allowances.

- Embroidery stitching is indicated on the templates in red. Directions for which embroidery stitches to use are provided with the block instructions.

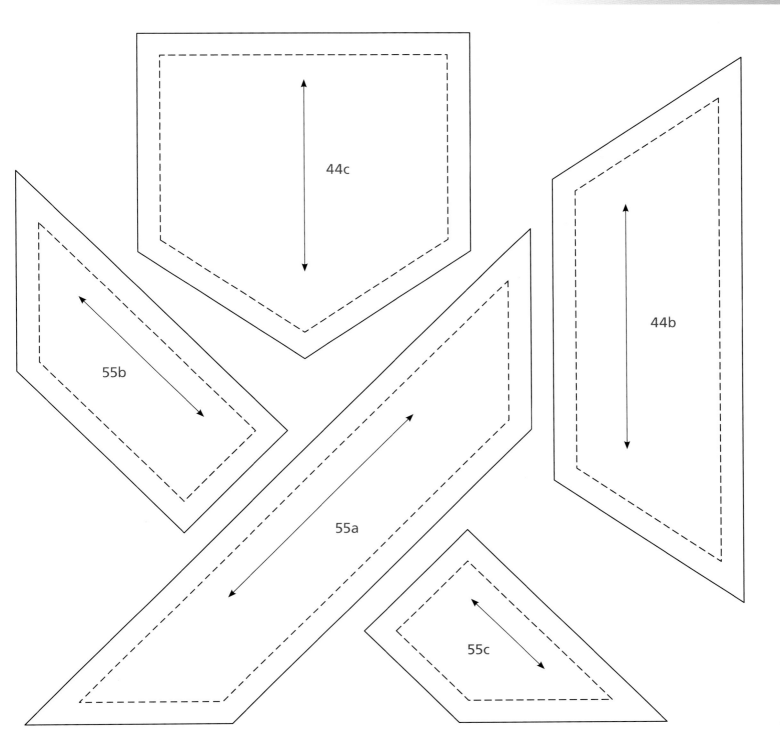

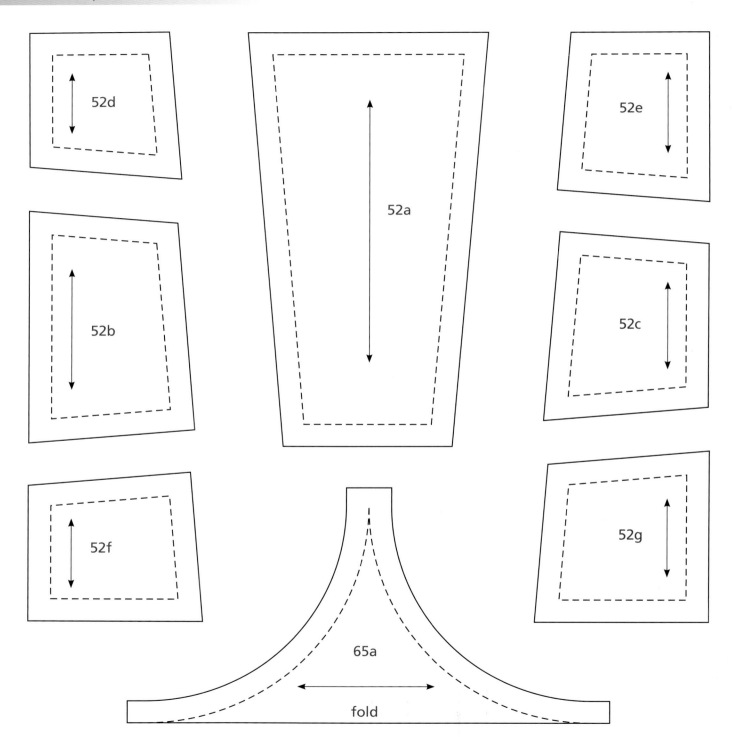

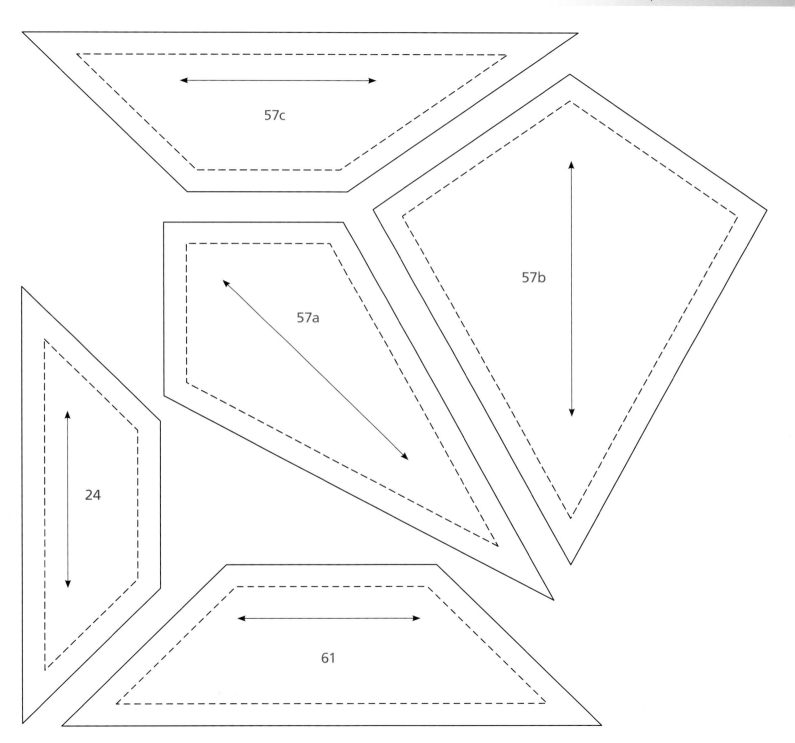

57c

57b

57a

24

61

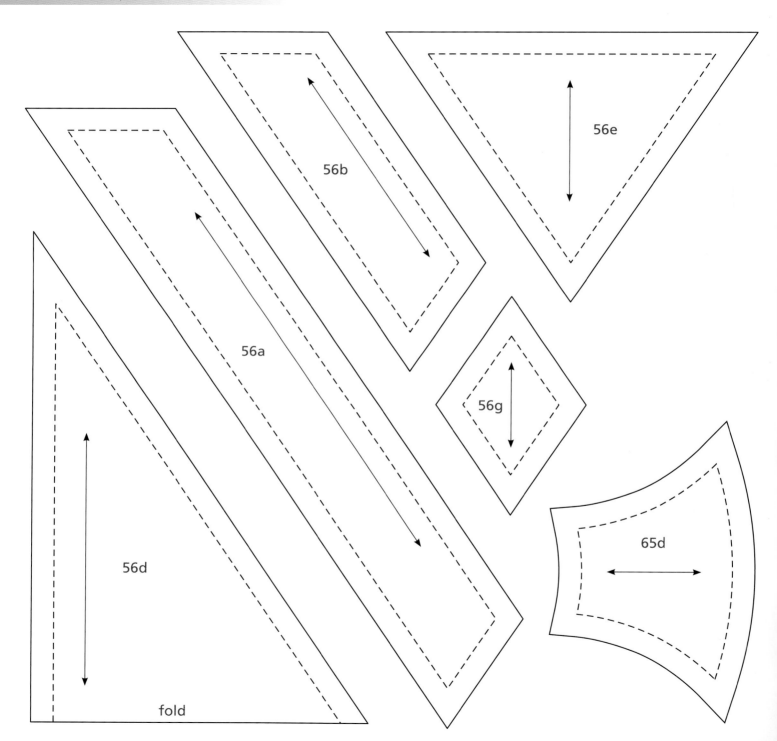

56b

56e

56a

56d

56g

65d

fold

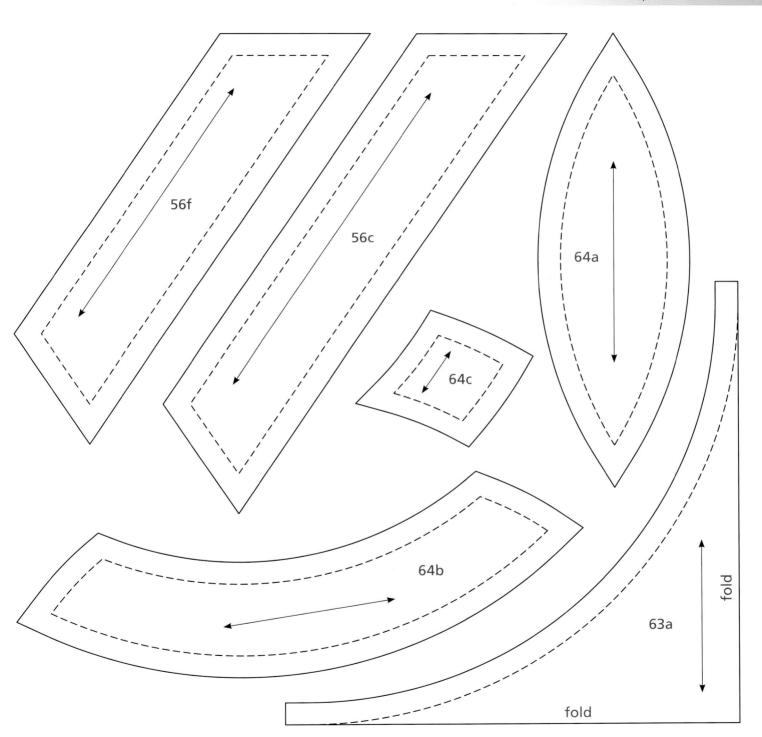

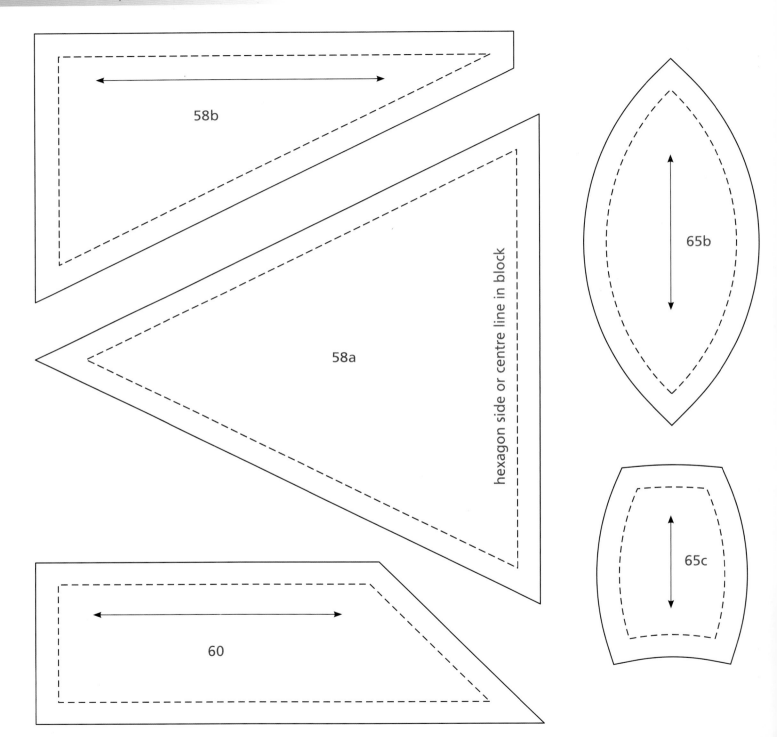

58b

58a

hexagon side or centre line in block

60

65b

65c

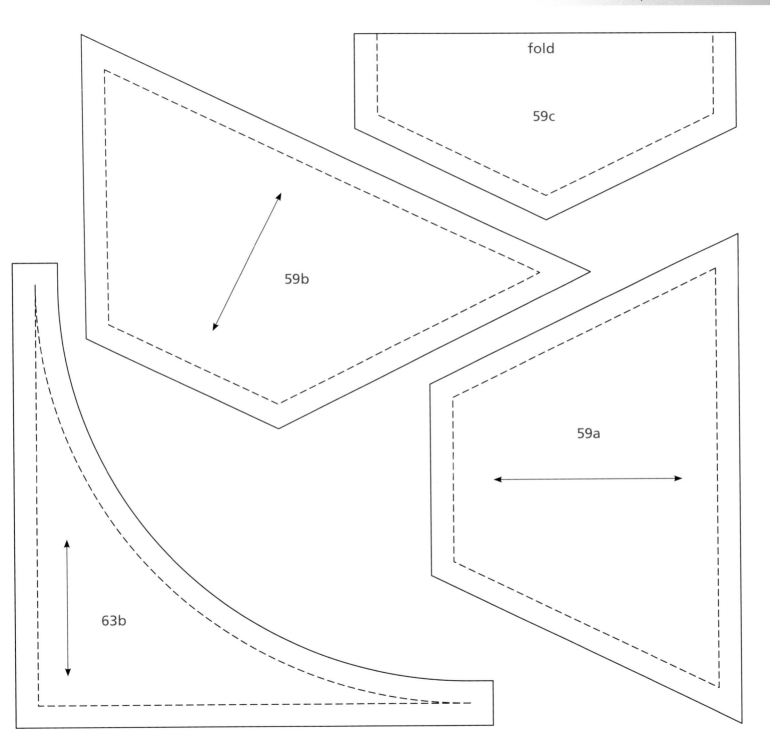

fold

59c

59b

59a

63b

The templates on pages 116–122 are for appliqué blocks 66–105.

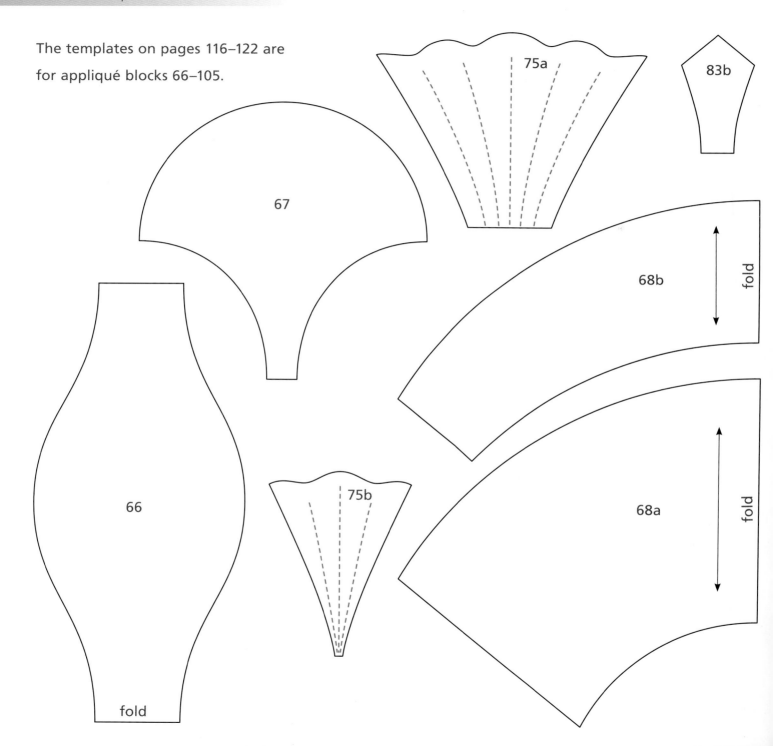

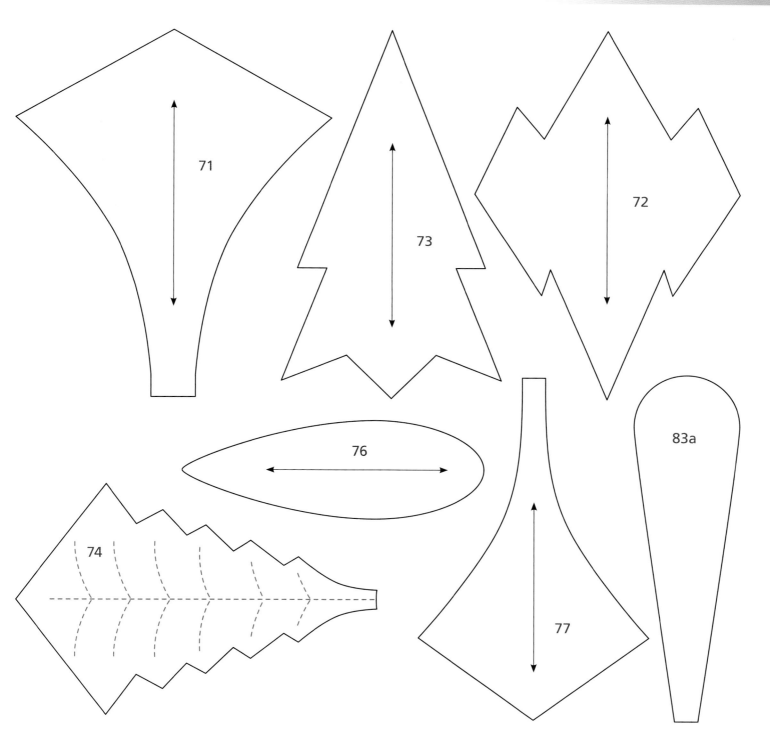

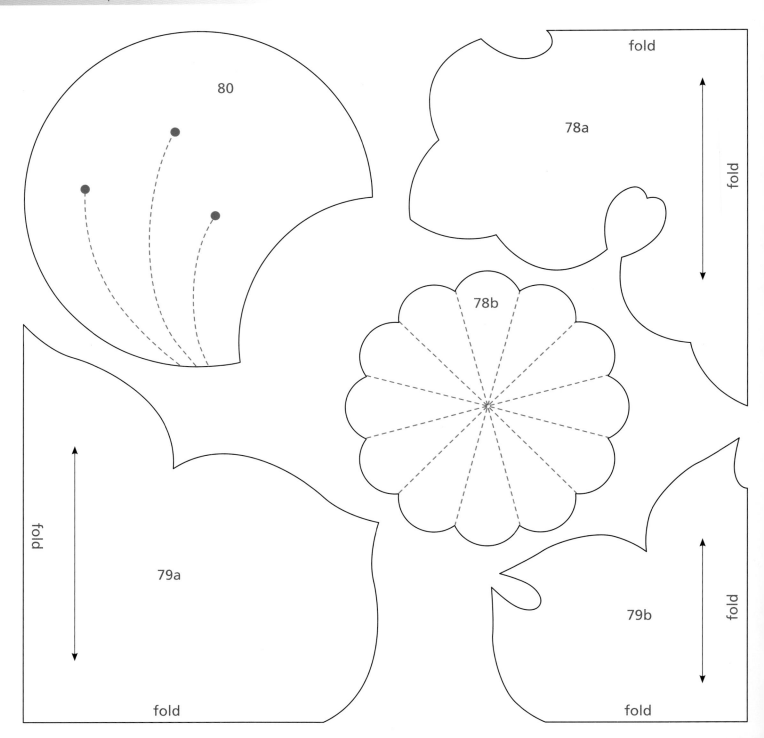

80

fold

78a

fold

78b

fold

79a

fold

79b

fold

fold

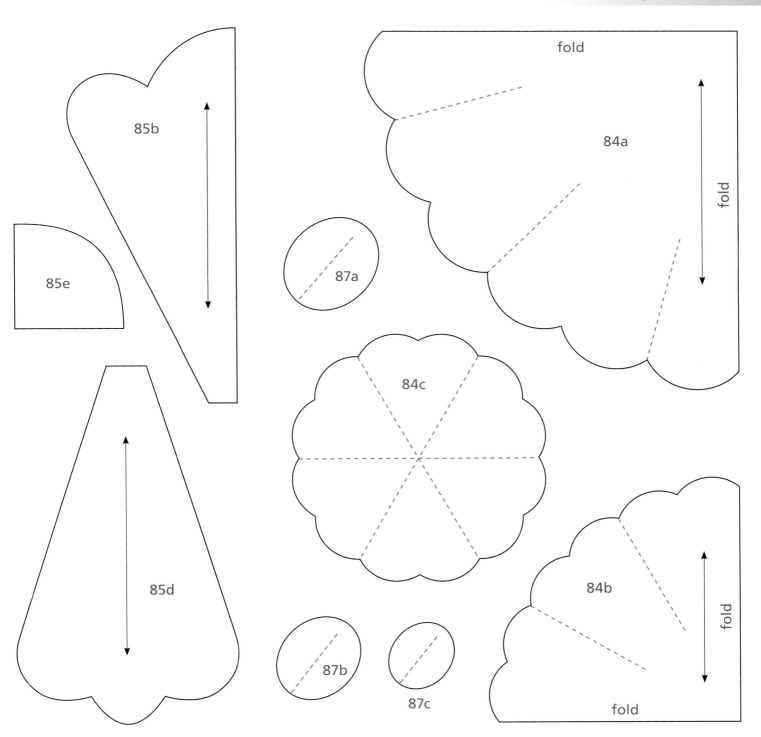

85b

85e

85d

fold

84a

fold

87a

84c

fold

84b

fold

87b

87c

fold

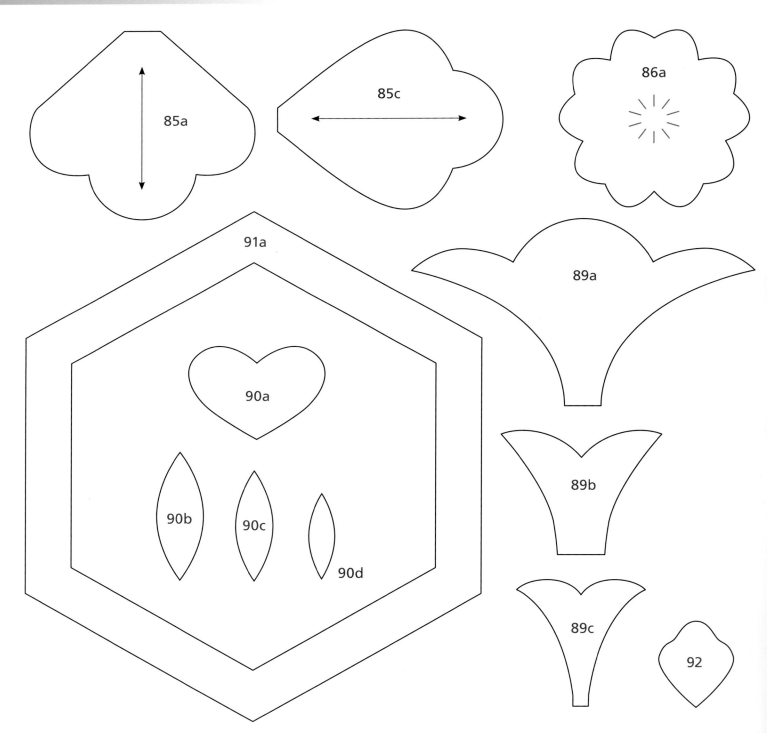

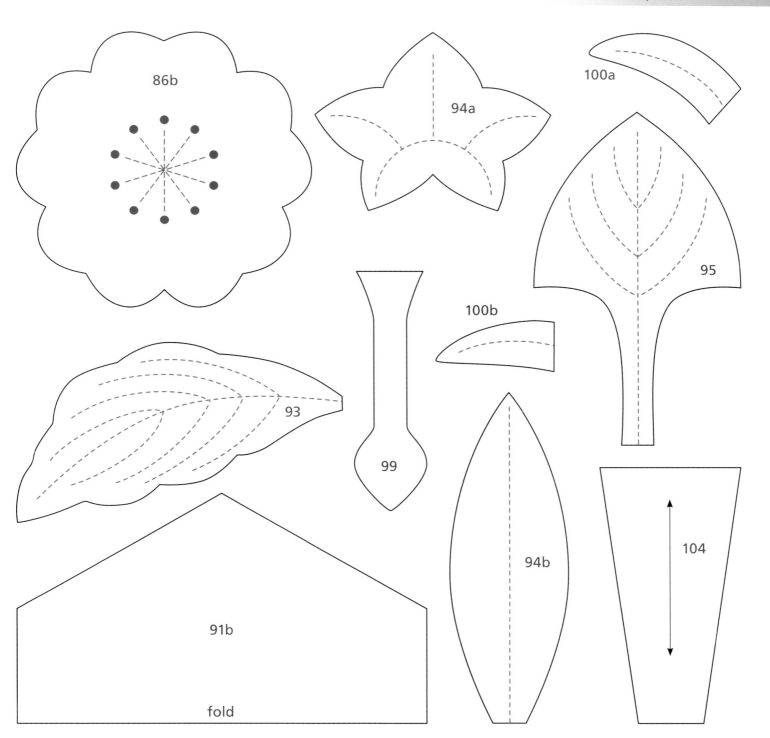

86b

94a

100a

95

93

100b

99

94b

104

91b

fold

The templates on pages 123–126 are for combined technique blocks 106–125. The black dots on templates 107, 108 and 109 relate to the sewing sequence explained in the main block instructions.

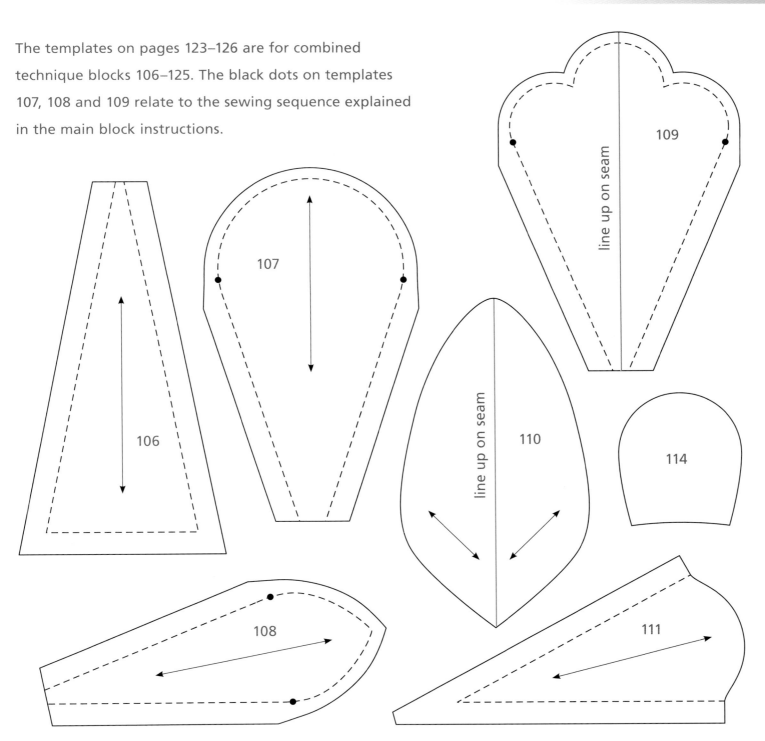

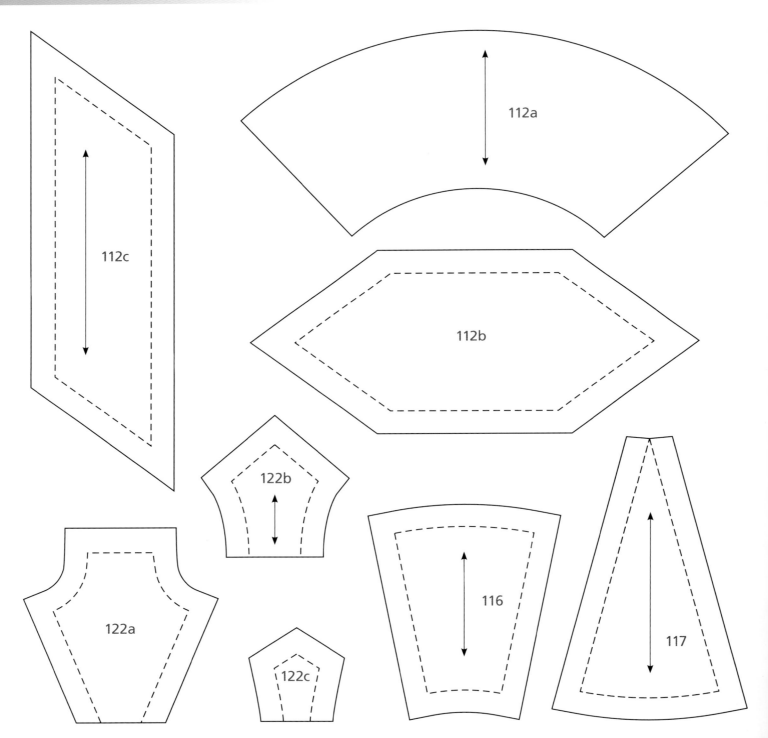

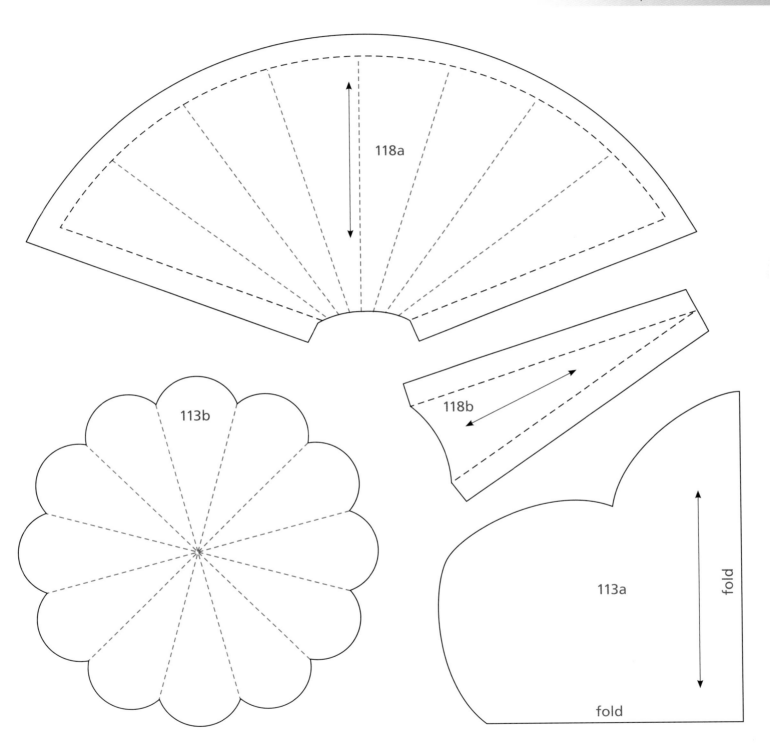

118a

113b

118b

113a

fold

fold

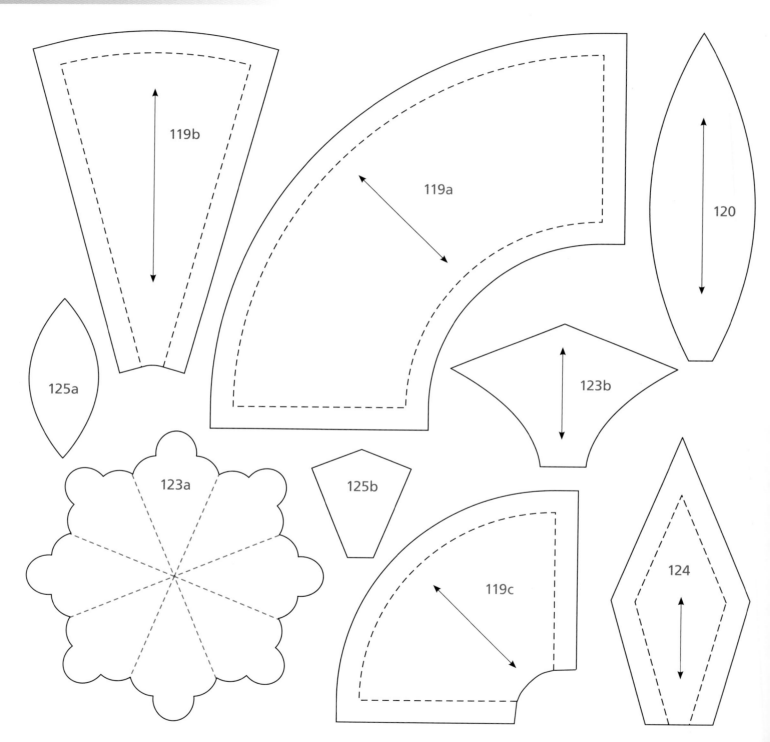

Index

Resources and credits

Suppliers

UNITED KINGDOM
Antique Angel
36 Denham Lane
Chalfont St Peter
Gerrards Cross SL9 0ET
Tel: 077-6588-8136
orders@antiqueangel.co.uk
www.antiqueangel.co.uk
*Japanese taupes and quilting
supplies (mail order and shop)*

The Cotton Patch
1283–1285 Stratford Road
Hall Green, Birmingham B28 9AJ
Tel: 0121-702-2840
mailorder@cottonpatch.co.uk
www.cottonpatch.co.uk
*Japanese taupes and quilting
supplies (mail order and shop)*

Euro Japan Links Ltd
32 Nant Road
Childs Hill
London NW2 2AT
Tel: 020-8201-9324
eurojapanlinks@aol.com
www.eurojapanlinks.co.uk
*Japanese textiles, patchwork
and sashiko supplies (mail order)*

Patchwork Corner
51 Belswains Lane
Hemel Hempstead
Hertfordshire HP3 9PW
Tel: 01442-259-000
www.patchworkcorner.co.uk
*Japanese taupes and quilting
supplies (mail order and shop)*

Quiltessential
Arkwright's Mill
Mill Road
Cromford
Derbyshire DE4 3RQ
Tel: 01629-825-936
www.quiltessential.co.uk
*Japanese taupes and quilting
supplies (mail order and shop)*

Susan Briscoe Designs
Yamadera
4 Mount Zion
Brymbo
Wrexham LL11 5NB
susan@susanbriscoe.co.uk
www.susanbriscoe.co.uk
*Vintage Japanese fabrics
(mail order)*

UNITED STATES
Debsews Fabrics
P.O. Box 161285
Honolulu, HI 96816
Tel: 808-221-5055
debsews123@yahoo.com
www.debsews2.com
*Japanese taupes and prints
(mail order)*

eQuilter.com
5455 Spine Road, Suite E
Boulder, CO 80301
Tel: (USA toll free) 877-322-7423
or 303-527-0856
service@eQuilter.com
www.eQuilter.com
*Fabrics and quilting supplies
(mail order)*

Hancock's of Paducah
3841 Hinkleville
Paducah, KY 42001
Tel: 800-845-8723 or
(international) 1-270-443-4410
customerservice@
hancocks-paducah.com
www.hancocks-paducah.com
*Fabric and quilting supplies
(mail order)*

Homestead Hearth
105 N. Coal Street
Mexico, MO 65265
Tel: 573-581-1966
info@homesteadhearth.com
www.homesteadhearth.com
*Japanese taupes and other fabrics
(mail order and shop)*

Jo-Ann Fabric and Craft Stores
5555 Darrow Road
Hudson, OH 44236
Tel: 888-739-4120
www.joann.com
*Fabrics and quilting supplies
(mail order and shops nationwide;
website features store locator)*

Pinwheels
2006 Albany Post Road
Croton-on-Hudson, NY 10520
Tel: 914-271-1045
www.pinwheels.com
*Japanese taupes and other fabrics
(mail order and shop)*

CANADA
Kallisti Quilts
Tel: 519-569-8718
michelle@kallistiquilts.com
www.kallistiquilts.com
*Japanese taupes and other fabrics
(mail order)*

Author's acknowledgements

I would like to thank my family,
my quilting friends, the quilt
shops listed in the Suppliers section
for all their assistance sourcing
fabrics, Clover for their lovely
bias tape and handy gadgets,
and Bernina – my 153 Quilter's
Edition sewing machine stitched
everything beautifully; and finally,
many thanks to all the team at
Quarto for producing another
beautiful book.